YOU CAN TEACH YOURSELF®
DULCIMER

by
Madeline MacNeil

AUDIO CONTENTS

1	Introduction and Tuning [1:32]
2	Strumming In Rhythm [:53]
3	Strumming In Rhythm 2 [1:01]
4	Strumming In Rhythm 3 [:56]
5	Strumming Exercises [1:08]
6	Strumming Exercises 2 [:46]
7	Strumming Exercises 3 [:28]
8	Are You Sleeping? [1:20]
9	Boil That Cabbage Down [1:06]
10	Boil That Cabbage Down 2 [:40]
11	Boil That Cabbage Down 3 [1:03]
12	Boil That Cabbage Down 4 [1:22]
13	Waterbound [1:29]
14	Soldier's Joy [1:53]
15	Cripple Creek [3:15]
16	John Brown's Dream [2:24]
17	Down in the Valley [2:20]
18	Ode to Joy [1:15]
19	O Suzanna [1:00]
20	Ode to Joy 2 [:27]
21	Au Clair De La Lune [1:01]
22	Flop Eared Mule [2:21]
23	Golden Slippers [3:15]
24	Simple Gifts [1:14]
25	Amazing Grace [:53]
26	She'll Be Coming 'Round the Mountain [1:11]
27	Home on the Range [1:10]
28	When Johnny Comes Marching Home [:50]
29	Away in a Manger [2:09]
30	The Ash Grove [1:23]
31	Arkansas Traveler [1:52]
32	Shady Grove [1:20]
33	Greensleeves [1:23]
34	The Willow Song [1:18]
35	Going to Boston [:53]
36	Bonnie Tyneside [1:15]
37	She'll Be Coming 'Round the Mountain [:50]
38	Home on he Range [1:15]
39	When Johnny Comes Marching Home [1:53]
40	Whiskey Before Breakfast [1:32]
41	Harvest Home [1:56]
42	Harvest Home 2 [1:30]
43	Country Gardens [:58]
44	Ah, Poor Bird [1:37]
45	Lo, How a Rose E'er Blooming [2:22]
46	Lo, How a Rose E'er Blooming [2:40]

Online Audio & Video

Audio
www.melbay.com/94304EB

Video
dv.melbay.com/94304

YouTube
www.melbay.com/94304V

DEDICATION

This book is dedicated to my teachers James McCombs and Emily Clark; Jewel Magee, Millie Chaplin, Chuck Warnick, Bruce Henn, Sally Alford, Jim Mann, and other dulcimer students who enrich my life so much; and to Seth Austen, Lorraine Lee, Anna Barry, Lois Hornbostel, and Keith Young-music beneath my wings.

WWW.MELBAY.COM

Contents

About the Author

Madeline MacNeil has performed in concert and at festivals in most of the continental United States, both as a soloist and with her husband, Seth Austen, a fine acoustic guitarist. She is best known for her work as a singer and player of hammered and fretted dulcimers. Maddie has been on the faculty of the Augusta Heritage Arts Workshops (Elkins, West Virginia) and the Appalachian State University Dulcimer Workshop (Boone, North Carolina).

Her recordings include HEART'S EASE, CHRISTMAS COMES ANEW, SOON IT'S GOING TO RAIN and THE HOLLY AND THE IVY. A native of Virginia, Maddie is editor/publisher of DULCIMER PLAYERS NEWS, an international quarterly journal for players and builders of hammered and fretted dulcimers.

The artists whose delightful drawings appear in this book are Gerry Norris of Strathroy, Ontario, Canada, and R. P. Hale of Concord, New Hampshire.

Photo by Dale Blindheim

Introduction

Welcome to the world of the dulcimer! You have many reasons why you have chosen this delightful instrument to play, and I will try to respect the many directions from which you may approach playing it. If you want to play the dulcimer because you have never succeeded with the guitar, piano or another instrument, you are in luck. Played traditionally, the dulcimer sounds delightful with drones accenting the melody you are playing. After a few hours of study you can bring good sounds forth which will rival any instrument at the beginning level. If you want to express your feelings for Elizabethan music, Irish tunes or even bluegrass you are in luck. No matter what you may have ever heard, the dulcimer is not a toy or stringed kazoo. It is a serious, true musical instrument which stretches as far as your imagination. Think of your music-learning as a life-long adventure filled with insight and expression amid moments of frustration because you long for the new step which seems to refuse to come forth.

In this book you may find musical skills you didn't wish to find. In every venture in life we often secretly hope to find gifts . . . wisdom without sometimes painful growth, artistry without hours of cleaning the brushes that mysteriously try to frustrate us, and musical abilities without hours of practice. Even musical geniuses throughout the ages have struggled and practiced to achieve the expression they so desperately wanted. Perhaps your goals are those of relaxation rather than performance. That's fine and I encourage these goals. However, I hope you will still approach the musical skills, the chord practice and rhythmic exercises with the excitement which comes with the stretching of our minds.

You will find some musical notation to interpret and understand. There are fine music-reading instrument players who are totally lost when presented with improvisation. There are players by ear who say there is no need to read music. Both players are right in many ways. Music libraries are filled with written music, so why improvise? The air is filled with tunes to learn by ear, so why read music? I contend that a middle ground is the best place to be. Practice learning by ear and have the ability to sample the perhaps incredible, perhaps long-forgotten, tunes tucked away in books. Music as a written language has developed over hundreds of years. It tries to capture the spritely, the somber, the pensive musical ideas of people throughout the centuries. It is wonderful to be able to tap those ideas as well as the ideas transported through the minds, the ears and the mouths of people.

USING THIS BOOK: The lessons in this book follow learning concentrations such as melodic playing or chording. It could easily take several practice sessions to digest a lesson. Move at your own pace and don't be concerned. I encourage you to read instructions, study guides and directions. They are there to help you.

You can find dulcimers with three to six strings (sometimes eight strings) which range widely in size. It's almost impossible to have an instruction book covering all the stringing possibilities. Throughout this book I'll be writing about three- or four-string (double melody) dulcimers. Look at your dulcimer. Does it correspond to any of the illustrations below as far as strings go? Can you alter the stringing somewhat so it corresponds? As long as you have three equal-distance strings (some or all of the strings can be doubled), we're all right. If not, you can consider taking off one or more strings, adjust tunings, or find another book which fits your dulcimer better.

| 3 string | 4 string | 5 string | 6 string |

PERSONAL PREFERENCE: Most of my work is done with a three-string dulcimer. I've explored some four equal-distance string dulcimers also. I do not like the feel of doubled strings, unless they're all doubled. If you want to chord or, especially, fingerpick a lot with your dulcimer, consider removing one or more strings. Removing a string is not a final statement of purpose! You can always put it back on. At this point you are probably exploring your options and don't know if you want to fingerpick or not. In that case, work along with the stringing you now have and make a decision later.

I recommend that you change strings before we begin. To reach the pitches we'll use, a .022 wound string for the bass, a .013 string for the middle, and .012 for the melody string(s) should work with your instrument. Refer to the section on changing strings for more help.

One last thought before we begin. The best players of any musical instrument started from scratch at some point. They've faced moments of frustration and elation. They still do. You will also.

If You Decide to Take Private or Group Lessons
Preparing for the First Session

Approaching a new learning experience can produce insecurities along with the anticipation. Preparation can help. Following are some suggestions.

In addition to your instrument, bring (if possible):
1. Extra strings
2. Your pick collection
3. Any dulcimer books you might have
4. Notebook and pen
5. Tape recorder (preferably battery-operated)
6. A portable music stand

Wear something comfortable, preferably clothes "pre-tested" for dulcimer playing. Slippery fabric in a skirt or pants can make you play "catch-the-dulcimer" most of the evening. Women: Wear slacks or a long skirt.

To help with a slipping instrument, consider bringing two of the fabric softener pads (like Clingfree) which have gone through the dryer. You can put them on top of your knees under the dulcimer. I found a useful, non-slip dulcimer pad in the K-Mart automotive department! It's a fake chamois cloth that, cut in half, provides two lap pads. To produce the grip, be sure to rinse out the cloth and let it dry before using for the first time. Unfortunately, the cloth does not come in designer colors.

Lesson 1: Exploring the Dulcimer

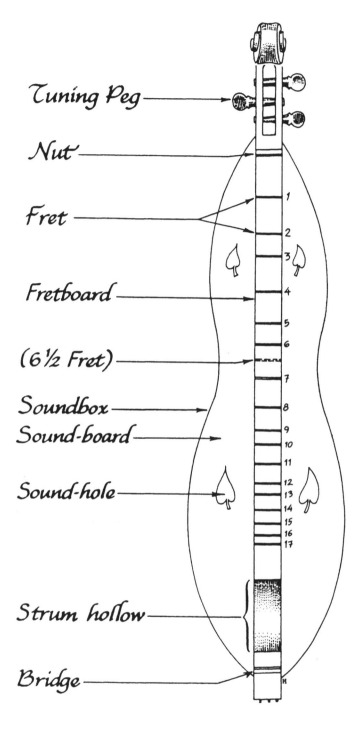

Tuning Peg

Nut

Fret

Fretboard

(6½ Fret)

Soundbox
Sound-board

Sound-hole

Strum hollow

Bridge

Before we begin tuning and playing, we'll explore your instrument to see the construction details. Dulcimers are usually hand-made and distinctly beautiful.

Look at the peg head. It will be apparent immediately whether you have metal tuners or the wooden tuners, often called friction pegs.

Look to the right of the bridge. If your dulcimer has fine tuners, each string will run through a kind of bead located to the right of the bridge. Fine tuners help you reach a precise tuning after you have turned the peg to get close.

Look at the center of the fretboard's length at the 6th fret. Do you see a cluster of four frets surrounding three fret spaces? If so, you have an extra fret, the one following the 6th fret. To keep everyone straight, we'll call the extra fret 6½. If you don't have the 6½ fret, don't worry. It is indeed an extra one which you can have added should you so desire. It permits the player to play more keys in one tuning. For now, if you have the extra fret, you may want to mark it with a bit of masking tape. But please don't physically number all of the frets. Learn them in the beginning so you won't have to depend on a "cheat sheet."

Please take a ruler and measure the fretboard from the nut to the bridge. This is called the vibrating string length (or scale length). In other words, it's that part of the string which is free to vibrate after it is stopped by the nut until it is stopped by the bridge. An average dulcimer has a vibrating string length of about 27 inches. Why should you measure the vibrating string length of your instrument? It's good to know about the dulcimer to begin with, but later this information will help you determine which strings to buy for your instrument. A player must become familiar with his or her dulcimer to bring forth its best sounds.

Dulcimer Problems

Sometimes there are problems which prevent the full enjoyment of a dulcimer. It's difficult to say to a student who has spent hard-earned money on an instrument that something should be fixed or changed. Yet it is easier to get something out in the open before frustration causes a potentially good player to hang the instrument on the wall and forget the whole thing. I hasten to add that there are many, many excellent builders; and chances are decidedly in your favor that your instrument is well made and will not give you problems. However, a builder cannot always anticipate the buyer's ultimate wishes in playing a dulcimer.

If a player chords when a builder made an instrument to be used with a noter, you may find the strings lie too high off the fretboard (action is too high). You can tell if your dulcimer has a too-high action in several ways. Obviously, if your favorite copy of GONE WITH THE WIND fits between the strings and the fretboard, you have a serious problem. Otherwise, if you have fretted tones which seem distorted, combined with a difficulty in depressing the strings, check things out with a good repair person. Lowering action is not difficult and shouldn't be costly at all unless the situation is compounded by a fretboard that isn't straight or by frets of uneven heights. Ask questions when you deal with a repair person. That's the best way to learn.

There are only small chances that you've purchased an inferior instrument that will need extensive work to make it playable. There are considerably more chances that you will have to adjust and modify your instrument to fit you and your style of playing. I've had minor adjustments made to most of my instruments, even to instruments that were expressly made for me.

Holding the Dulcimer

Find a low chair with a firm seat (no cushions) and without arms. The instrument should sit comfortably and firmly on your lap. Chair arms don't really permit this. Sofas encourage you to sit back—not good either. An apple crate makes a fine seat for dulcimer playing. Place the dulcimer comfortably on your lap—peg head to your left, bridge to your right. Angle the instrument by pushing the peg head end toward your left knee (the general area of the 3rd fret should be over your knee) and by pulling the bridge end toward your body. Press down any string at the 1st fret. Does the instrument tip? Readjust it on your lap, perhaps spreading your knees further apart. Comfortable? Let's begin.

Tuning

Most people approach tuning with the same dread with which they approach final exams in college or a visit to the dentist. I will try to make this as simple as possible while constantly reminding you that tuning becomes easier as time passes. Do not tell me you are tone deaf. As you tune the instrument and practice through the weeks, you'll organize tones and build musical skills. I know this may sound vague, but practice *does* help.

I encourage you to follow each tuning step—step by step—especially if you have tuning problems or still think you have a tin ear.

I'll name the dulcimer strings as follows:

BASS STRING: The farthest one from you, a heavy string.

MIDDLE STRING: The string between the bass and melody strings.

MELODY STRING(S): The string(s) closest to your body. We'll play melodies anywhere we wish, not only on the melody string, but I must call that string something! I'm avoiding numbers because we use them for too many other explanations.

Possibly the names of pitches or keys mean nothing to you. If that is the case, I suggest that for now you follow the directions as though some of the definitions made sense. Most of the problems will probably come with musical terms. A dictionary or music instruction book may be of help. We'll tune the dulcimer to the key of D (D below middle C on the bass string, A below middle C on the remaining strings) because most dulcimers can reach those pitches with no problems. Use a fixed pitch instrument. A pitch pipe or tuning fork is good. I like tuning forks, since my ears relate well to their sounds. But, it's not practical to carry around several, since one fork gives one tone. If you purchase a pitchpipe, get a chromatic one from a music store. It looks rather like a peppermint patty! I've seen them pitched from F above middle C to the octave above, but I suggest you get one from middle C to the octave above.

You'll have to become accustomed to octaves when you use a pitch pipe. When you blow D for tuning the bass string, you'll sound

(D above middle C). But you tune your bass string to the D below middle C.

I don't think this will trouble you too much. Simply think low! Should you use the D below middle C on a piano or the 4th (D) string of an in-tune guitar, you can sound the actual pitch for the bass string.

Before tuning each string, find the peg or tuner to which it is attached and determine which direction tightens the string (makes the pitch higher) or loosens it (makes the pitch lower).

WOODEN TUNING PEGS: As you tune higher (go slowly), push the peg into the peg head firmly (this doesn't mean with great force—just firmly). The turning and pushing motions should be done together. If you turn, find the pitch and <u>then</u> push the peg in, you might change the pitch slightly. Ordinary blackboard chalk can help both sticking and slipping wooden tuning pegs. For best results, use the chalk sparingly.

METAL TUNERS: You should find no real problems unless the tuner slips out of place when you've reached pitch. Find a small screwdriver (assuming the tuner has a screw) and tighten the tuner slightly. It's a good idea to keep a screwdriver in your pick case.

If you have a problem later reaching D on the bass string or if you have no fixed pitch tool, simply tune the bass string to a comfortable pitch (string is taut, but not ready to break at any second) and skip to STEP TWO in the tuning directions.

TUNING: STEP ONE

1. Loosen your bass string until it is somewhat floppy.
2. Sound D on the pitchpipe—long and steadily.
3. Listen and think about that tone.
4. Sound D again and hum it.
5. Pluck the bass string with your right thumb. Don't "twang" it. That makes it difficult to hear a real tone.
6. Reach over your dulcimer and tighten the peg or tuner with your right hand.
7. Repeat nos. 2 through 6 until the bass string reaches the desired pitch.
8. RULE: It is important to learn the response of your instrument. Wooden pegs usually go higher faster than metal tuners. Work slower with wooden pegs.
9. RULE: When tuning, sound the pitch you want, *then* the pitch you have on the string. This will help you keep the two tones straight in your mind. Follow this pattern consistently: Pitch you want, pitch you've got. Turn the tuning peg. Pitch you want, pitch you've got. Turn the tuning peg, etc.
10. SUGGESTION: Let your voice help you. If you don't know which of two pitches is high, hum each. That should help you.
11. SUGGESTION: To help you hear the tones, especially in a classroom situation, hold the dulcimer next to your ear.

TUNING: STEP TWO

1. "Open" is the unfretted string. Using your right hand thumb, pluck the open bass string.
2. Place any finger of your left hand just to the left of the first fret of the bass string and pluck with your right hand.
3. Slide your left hand finger to the left of the second fret and pluck with your right hand.
4. Repeat up to the fourth fret.
5. Repeat this entire sequence (open, 1st, 2nd, 3rd, 4th frets on the bass string) moving decisively from one fret to the next. You have just played the first five tones of a major scale (Do Re Mi Fa Sol). The actual tones you played are D, E, F#, G and A below middle C.
6. Pick out some tunes on the bass string, using the open string as home base. Try some nursery rhymes such as "Mary Had A Little Lamb" which begins at the 2nd fret.

TUNING: STEP THREE

We will use several tunings in this book, beginning with DAA. Please remember that no tuning is more magical or "mature" than another. You'll find your favorite tunings after you've played for awhile.

1. Sound the open bass string.
2. Sound the bass string at the 4th fret.
3. Repeat nos. 1 and 2 numerous times. You are getting the scale interval Do to Sol (D to A) in your mind.
4. Sing "Do—Sol" along with your playing.
5. Sing "Do—Sol" without playing.
6. Repeat nos. 4 and 5 several times.
7. If you need help, sing the "twinkle, twinkle" part of "Twinkle, Twinkle, Little Star". That song begins with a Do—Sol interval.
8. Your bass string is tuned to D (Do). Tune your middle string to A (Sol). Repeat any of the above numbers (especially no. 2) to help you along the way.

WARNING: Strangely enough, sometimes when a string is pitched higher than we want, it actually sounds lower! If you're tuning higher, the string is getting very tight and you still seem far away from the note you want, loosen the string considerably until you *know* you're below the pitch you want and start over.

TUNING: STEP FOUR

When the middle string is tuned, tune the melody string(s) to the same pitch as the middle string, using Step Three, no. 3 to help you if necessary. If the tuning process has been difficult for you, don't despair. Time does help. Also helpful are a quiet place in which to work, patience (walk away from the instrument awhile if you get frustrated) and no distracting sounds, particularly musical sounds such as a stereo or radio.

Exploring the Tuned Dulcimer

I've said that Do (or D in this case) is located on the open bass string. That is the lowest tone of your dulcimer. But there are higher tones also, among them more "Do's". Compare the tone at the 3rd fret of the melody string with the open bass string. That tone should be one octave higher than the tone on the bass string.

D—Open bass
string

D—3rd fret
melody string

Scale Exercise

Play the following tones:

BASS STRING   Open, 1st, 2nd, 3rd frets

MELODY STRING: Open string through the 10th fret

You have just played a two octave scale in the key of D which looks like the following in musical notation.

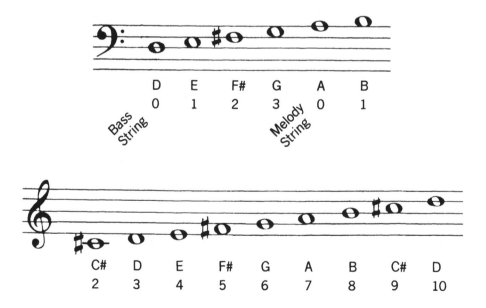

PLEASE NOTE: Whenever I say, "Play the (whatever number) fret", that is a shorter way of saying, "Play just to the left of the (whatever number) fret".

You probably had a few more frets after the 10th fret, so you could actually have gone higher. At the moment, your middle and melody strings are tuned to the same pitch. When the time comes to change your tuning scheme, you'll have even more notes available.

Strumming

We will study rhythmic notation in some depth. Finding the right notes is not all that difficult. Playing rhythmically can be. We will try to skip over some stumbling blocks by starting at the beginning.

If you like math, you are in luck. Rhythmic notation is simply that: mathematics. Remember your elementary school teacher saying, "You have an apple. You cut it into two halves to share with a friend. Two more friends come along and you cut each half once more so that you have four quarters...". A time signature at the beginning of a written piece of music sets the scene for a similar story. Example: The common time signature of 4/4. The top number means there are four beats in a measure. The bottom number tells what note gets one beat (in this case a quarter note).

measure   measure

Rhythmic notation is relative to the time signature. 6/8 time means that an eighth note gets one beat and there are six beats per measure. Therefore, the *value* of a note can change, but the *relationship* of one note to another remains the same. A quarter note can be worth one beat in one tune and two beats in another. BUT it always takes two quarter notes to equal the value of a half note, two eighth notes to equal the value of a quarter note, and so forth.

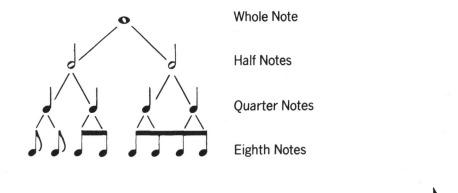

Whole Note

Half Notes

Quarter Notes

Eighth Notes

Eighth notes are written in two ways depending on how they're used. A single eighth note is drawn 𝄾 .

When you have two eighth notes, they can be drawn 𝄾 𝄾 or 𝅘𝅥𝅮𝅘𝅥𝅮 . As you can see, the latter

way of presenting two eighth notes is less cluttered.

RULE: There must *always* be the correct number of beats per measure as indicated by the time signature. The only exception (and it's not really an exception) is the first and last measures. Sometimes the music has a note or two to kick off the tune. Think of "The Star-Spangled Banner" which begins, "Oh, say can you see...". The two notes on the word "Oh" simply prepare you for the first full measure which begins with the word "say". If the music is written correctly, the last measure of such a tune will be incomplete also, but if you add the number of beats in the "kick-off" measure and the last measure, you will have the exact number of beats for a complete measure as indicated in the time signature.

Practice strumming across the strings a few times. Don't cramp your arm and wrist for a "dainty" strum. Strum with your entire arm (from the elbow down) combined with a flexible wrist.

Picks

Your pick must feel comfortable. If the pick is too short and heavy, it might be difficult to strum with freedom of movement. A dulcimer class is a wonderful place to play "Pass the Pick". Strum a little with your neighbor's pick and pass picks around until yours returns. Your teacher will have ideas about various picks. Some picks seem to produce more strumming noise than others and would be ones to avoid. Varieties include numerous shapes and sizes and weights from thin to extra heavy.

As always, keep an open mind. Search music or folk stores and when you find picks you like, buy a good supply.

The Strumming Area

It would be natural that the spot to strum is over the strum hollow. This is not necessarily so. Notice the different sounds you achieve when strumming close to the bridge, in the middle of the strum hollow and then over the fretboard, somewhere close to the 10th fret. Eventually you will want to use all strumming areas for interpretation and effect. For now, I suggest you strum over the fretboard. This gives your right hand a good position and sweetens the tone somewhat.

Strum Direction

When you strum, you interpret the rhythmic note values. Music must be rhythmically strong, therefore, a strong strumming pattern is a must. Strong, by the way, doesn't necessarily mean loud. You can strum toward you (in-strum) or away from you (out-strum), but one action must dominate over the other. You will find good dulcimer players whose dominant strumming action is the in-strum. Other good dulcimer players have a dominant out-strum. People who play instruments like the guitar tend to have dominant out-strums. Old-time dulcimer players tend to have a dominant in-strum. You'll hear arguments for both—and the ultimate decision is up to you. I've found in teaching dozens of students that the out-strum seems to present less coordination problems. (I have no scientific studies to back me up, just observations). Therefore, I will teach you the out-strum. If you wish to do otherwise, simply reverse everything I say!

Strumming in Rhythm

We'll begin by strumming quarter notes that receive one beat in measures that contain four beats (look at the time signature). This arrow ↑ means an out-strum.

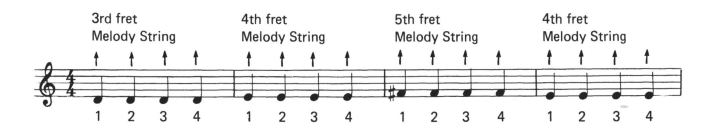

As you can see, that gets old in a hurry. Music, naturally, would have put us all to sleep centuries ago if every note had the same value. Let's add in some eighth notes for variety. To count out loud, we need another word to fill in with the numbers. Count 1 2 & 3 4. RULE: On each of the primary beats (1, 2, 3, 4) do an out-strum. On the off-beats (what we call "ands" here), do an in-strum.

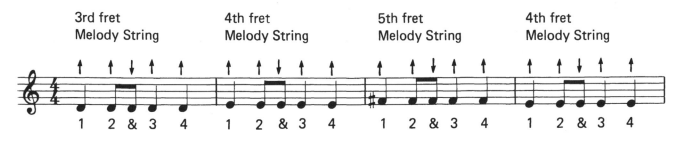

In the example below we'll add in more eighth notes for a count of 1 2 & 3 4 &.

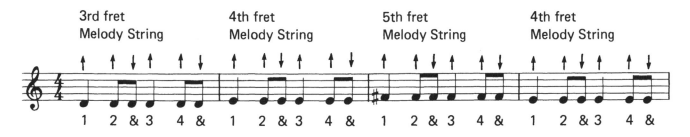

If rhythm is difficult for you, picture marching around a room - left, right, left, right - counting 1, 2, 3, 4. If you add in some running steps - still keeping time - you'll have walk, running, walk, walk (1 2 & 3 4) or walk, running, walk, running (1 2 & 3 4 &) or some other combination. Consider half notes as a spot to step and wait before stepping again.

Strumming Exercises

Right hand: Strum
Left hand: use index, middle ring and/
or little fingers walking or sliding to each fret.

I

Tuning: DAA for all

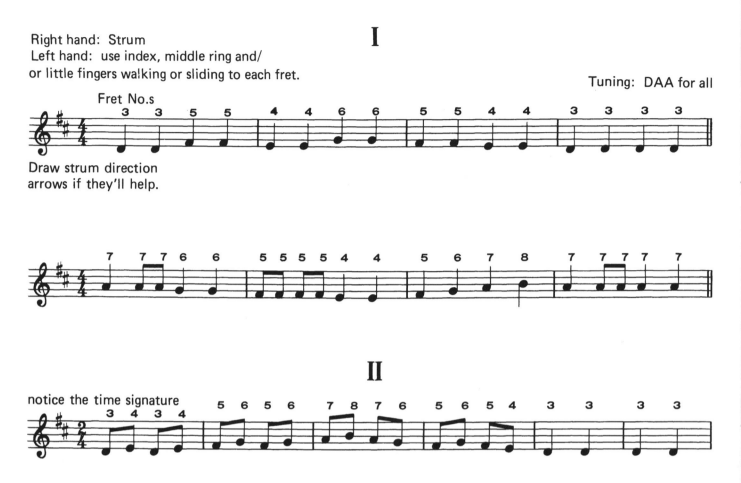

Fret No.s

Draw strum direction
arrows if they'll help.

II

notice the time signature

PLAYING HINT TO REMEMBER: When you're playing one fret, then going to the next higher or lower fret, and returning to the original fret, let two left hand fingers help you. For example, in the first measure of the exercise II, place your middle finger at the 3rd fret. Reach out with the index finger to the 4th fret. LEAVE YOUR MIDDLE FINGER WHERE IT IS AT THE 3rd FRET. YES, TWO OR MORE FINGERS ON ANY STRING IS ALL RIGHT. When returning to the 3rd fret, all you have to do is lift your index finger. Please remember this technique, as it will give further stability to your left hand fingering.

III

notice the time signature

A SPECIAL NOTE TO OUR LEFT-HANDED FRIENDS: In reality, it seems that the dulcimer was made for you. Most of the intricate, difficult work is done by your dominant left hand. I recommend that you keep the regular dulcimer stringing with the peg head to your left along with everyone else. Then you should feel compassion for us right-handed folks who struggle to make our left hands cooperate.

TUNE INTERPRETATION: We're now all right when it comes to eighth and quarter notes. But what about the longer notes, primarily half and whole notes? This is the place for some interpretation and playing by ear. When you strum a dulcimer, the sound begins to die away immediately. If you strum just once for one of those long-valued notes, the sound will probably be gone long before it's time to strum the next note. Later in this book we'll work with a combination of picking and strumming which is often used with slower, chorded tunes. You'll then see tunes where half notes are held, not filled in. But faster, strummed tunes almost always need filling in for the longer notes.

RULE: This doesn't hold true for the final note in a tune. That should be strummed and allowed to die away.

ANOTHER RULE: If you're going to play a tune more than once, a long note at the end should be filled in with strums until you've played it for the last time.

If you have a half note, you can divide it into: 2 quarter notes, a quarter note and 2 eighth notes, 2 eighth notes and a quarter note, or 4 eighth notes along with more complex combinations. Try your wings on filling out the half notes in measures 3, 4 and 7 in the following tune. The half note in measure 8 should be strummed and held the last time the tune is played. I suggest you draw strum direction arrows where they will be helpful.

Are You Sleeping?

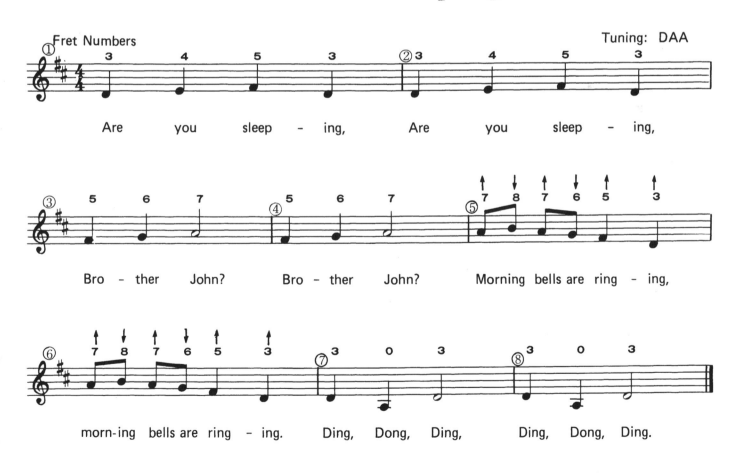

TO PLAY AS A ROUND: Each new voice enters as the voice ahead reaches measure 3.

Reading Tablature

As you grow in playing the dulcimer, you'll probably study tunes in other books. Sooner or later you'll find tablature to read. Rather than wait until later, we'll begin with tablature now. I consider musical notation and tablature to work together, and you'll find both in this book.

Tablature presents a rather specific picture of your dulcimer fretboard -- three lines for the three strings. Musical notation is written on five lines.

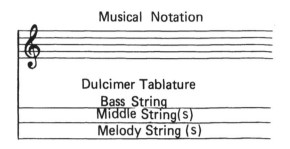

Numbers stand for frets (O stands for the open string). The top line represents the bass string, the middle line represents the middle string and the bottom line represents the melody strings(s).

Below, in example one you place a finger at the fifth fret of the melody string and keep the other strings open (unfretted). Example two requests that you place a finger at the third fret of the melody string and another finger at the second fret of the bass string.

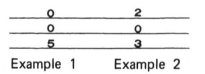

Example 1   Example 2

Sometimes tablature is written in a kind of shorthand. The playing instructions will say strum, but you only see a fret number on the bottom line of the tablature. The writer simply chooses not to write in all the zeros (for open strings) on the top and middle lines. The key word in the instruction is "strum".

Rhythmic indications in tablature look just like the musical notation.

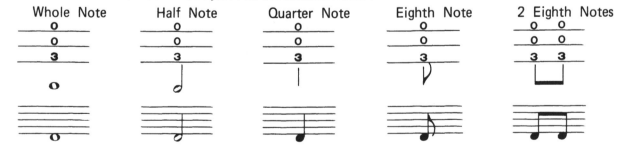

EXAMPLE OF TABLATURE ATTACHED TO MUSICAL NOTATION

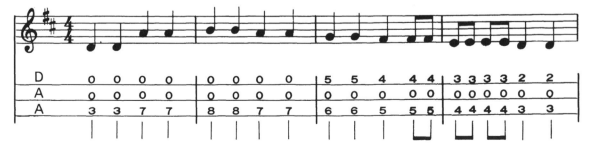

16

Fingering

Many of the tunes in this book will not have fingering marked in. I've anticipated several spots where fingering suggestions may save you time in working out a tune. They may also help you play smoother and with more ease.

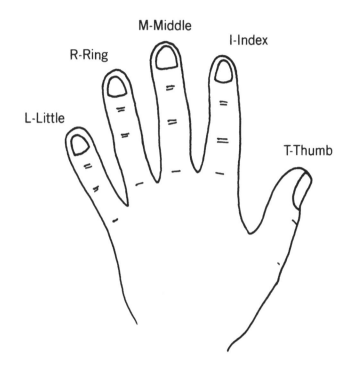

When you learn from written music or tablature, I suggest you "map out" your way first. Write fingerings down when you figure them out (especially later on when you find more complex movements). I also encourage you to consider changing the fingering when a passage in a tune just won't work out. Awkward fingering can interrupt the flow. One last thing: fingering should be fluid and rather simple. In other words, if your fingers are wrapped around your wrist while executing part of a tune, change the fingering!

When playing, keep your fingers close to the frets for a clearer tone. This doesn't mean on top of the frets, which won't give you much tone at all.

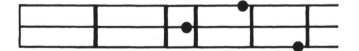

Boil That Cabbage Down

Old American Song

First:

1. Notice the time signature.
2. Look at the beginning of the tablature to see what tuning is used.
3. Count out the rhythm.
4. Notice measure 7. Melodically it is not the same as the others.
5. Notice measure 8. The last time you play the tune you strum for the half note and then allow
   the sound to die away. If you're repeating the tune, fill in that space with
   eighth and/or quarter notes.

FINGERING: Index and/or middle fingers, left hand.

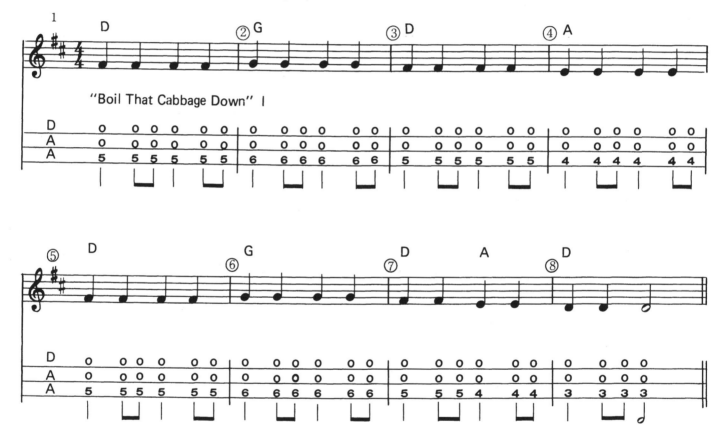

"Boil That Cabbage Down" I

When more than one player work on a tune, it's nice to have one person playing a harmony.
Following is a simple harmony which sounds good played with versions I, III, or IV of "Boil That
Cabbage Down".

Always feel free to draw in strum direction arrows if they'll help you.

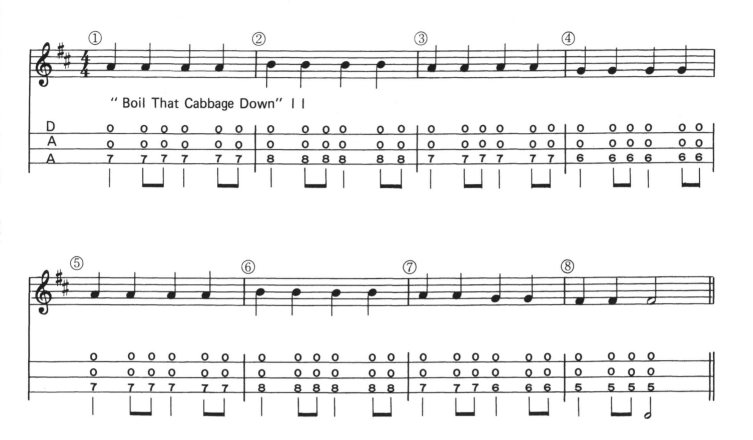

Version III uses a bass string harmony. FINGERING: Thumb on melody string, index finger on the bass string.

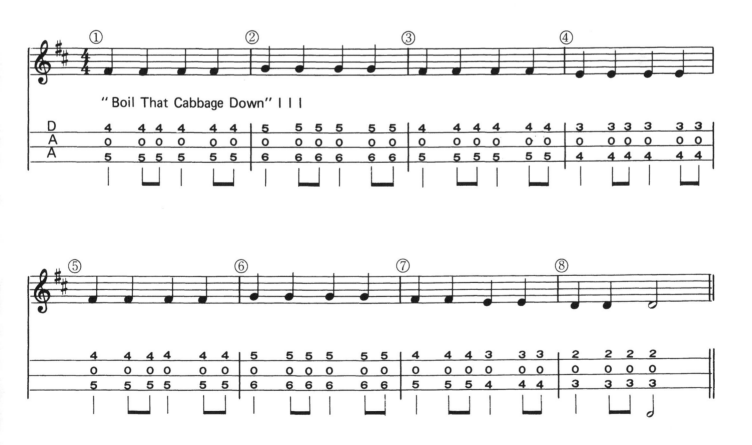

19

Version IV uses a middle string harmony. FINGERING: Thumb on melody string, Ring finger on middle string. Notice measure 8. To prevent a strange chord on the last measure, the middle string is left open.

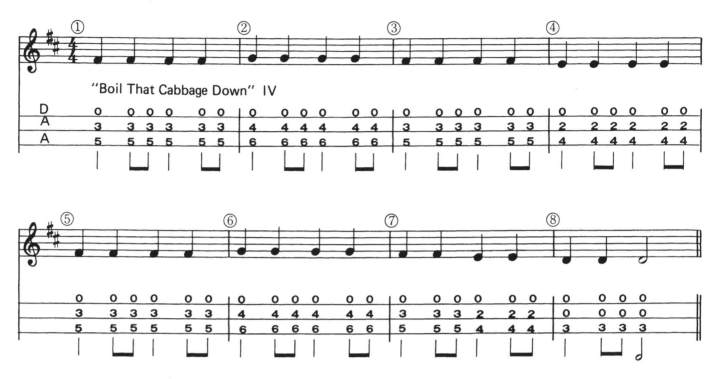

"Boil That Cabbage Down" IV

1. Boil that cabbage down boys,
   Bake them hoecakes brown.
   The only song that I can sing is
   Boil that cabbage down.

2. Raccoon has a bushy tail,
   The possum's tail is bare.
   The rabbit's got no tail at all,
   Just a tiny bunch of hair.

3. Possum's up a 'simmon tree,
   The raccoon's on the ground.
   Raccoon says to the possum,
   Please shake them 'simmons down.

Waterbound

Southern Virginia Song

Tempo: Moderately fast

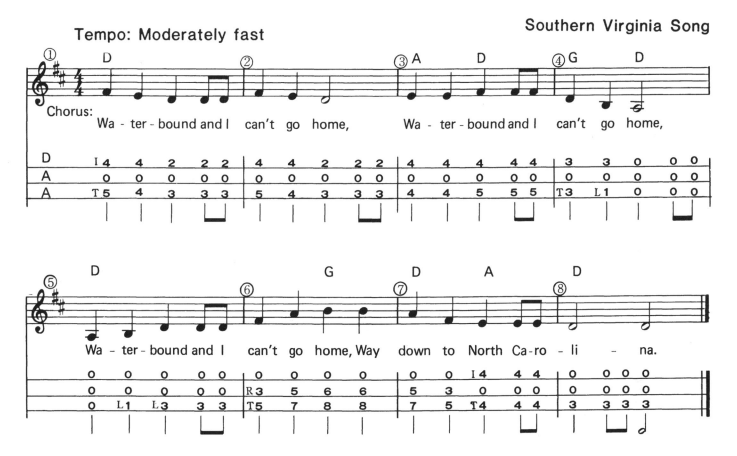

CHORUS

Waterbound and I can't go home,
Waterbound and I can't go home,
Waterbound and I can't go home,
Way down to North Carolina.

1. Chickens a - crowing in the old plowed field
   Chickens a - crowing in the old plowed field
   Chickens a - crowing in the old plowed field
   Way down in North Carolina.
   Chorus:

2. Water's up and I can't get across
   Water's up and I can't get across
   Water's up and I can't get across
   Gonna ride my old white horse.
   Chorus:

3. Old man's mad and I don't care
   Old man's mad and I don't care
   Old man's mad and I don't care
   As long as I get his daughter.
   Chorus:

4. If he don't give her up we're gonna run away
   If he don't give her up we're gonna run away
   If he don't give her up we're gonna run away
   Way down to North Carolina.
   Chorus:

5. Me and Tom and Joe's going home
   Me and Tom and Joe's going home
   Me and Tom and Joe's going home
   Way down to North Carolina.
   Chorus:

I learned this delightful song from Ralph Lee Smith. The chorus follows each verse.
As always, if you're playing the tune more than once, fill in the half note in measure 8
until the last time through.

Playing Hint: You may experience some problems getting the melody and harmony together while juggling the
rhythmic notation! If so, play just the melody, which is located on the bottom line of the tablature, keeping the
other strings open. When the melody is rooted in your memory, try the arrangement as written. If you play
and sing all of the verses later, vary what is going on in the accompaniment by playing some verses with
melody and open strings, others with the written arrangement. The variation will be nice.

Soldier's Joy

A special objective for this tune is light, dancing fingers plus more familiarity with the upper frets. I know you're still new at this, but I hope you'll return to "Soldier's Joy" frequently, lightening your touch so the tune dances. If you have much trouble, the action on your dulcimer might be too high or perhaps the double melody strings (should you have them) are bothering you.

Fingering: (Important). Use only the index, middle, and ring fingers. Get in the habit early of leaving fingers down, as anchors of sorts, while you play other notes.

Practice:

        Sliding (example—measure 2)

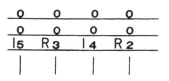

Enjoy the "whooshing" sound you'll hear. It's part of the music.

        Walking (example—measure 15)

In playing measure 15, put two fingers (ring and index) down at the 5th and 3rd frets. Play them as the music indicates. Slide your ring finger to the 2nd fret, drop your index finger at the 4th fret (you now have two fingers down again) and play as the music indicates. Learning and feeling comfortable with this movement is important for your left hand work.

Playing hints for SOLDIER'S JOY
1. The fast tempo does not mean the first time you play the tune! It could take you several weeks to work up your speed. The important thing is that it be played steadily at a comfortable tempo.
2. I decided to move the B part down an octave because I like the sound. However, the musical notation is written in the original octave so your fiddle-playing, music-reading friend can join you.
3. This may be your first encounter with repeat signs ‖: :‖, but it won't be your last. Fiddle and dance tunes usually follow a form of AABB which means Melody A, Melody A Repeated, Melody B, Melody B Repeated. To save space in books, repeated melodies are usually written only once with the direction to repeat. When you reach some dots :‖ at the end of a phrase, go back and look for dots going the other way ‖:. If you don't find any, return to the beginning and repeat the phrase. Walking through "Soldier's Joy", that means: Play measures 1-8. At the repeat sign in measure 8, go back to the beginning and repeat measures 1-8. Play measures 9-16. At the repeat sign in measure 16, go back to measure 9 and play until you reach measure 16 again.

Soldier's Joy

Playing Hint: Whenever you play melodies without chords, use only the index, middle, ring, and little fingers of your left hand. To involve your thumb, you have to turn your hand. This can sometimes hamper the musical lilt you're trying to achieve.

Cripple Creek/John Brown's Dream

The next two tunes are fun. Not only are they individually nice, you can play them together with a dulcimer friend in a kind of duet.

The individual tunes should work out fairly easily. Be sure to lean into the bass string somewhat in JOHN BROWN'S DREAM to bring out the melody. Measure 8 in CRIPPLE CREEK is a little tricky. Draw strum direction arrows if you need them.

When playing the tunes together, repeats are critical. The person doing CRIPPLE CREEK plays it through completely (with all repeats) THREE TIMES while the JOHN BROWN'S DREAM person plays that through TWICE with all repeats.

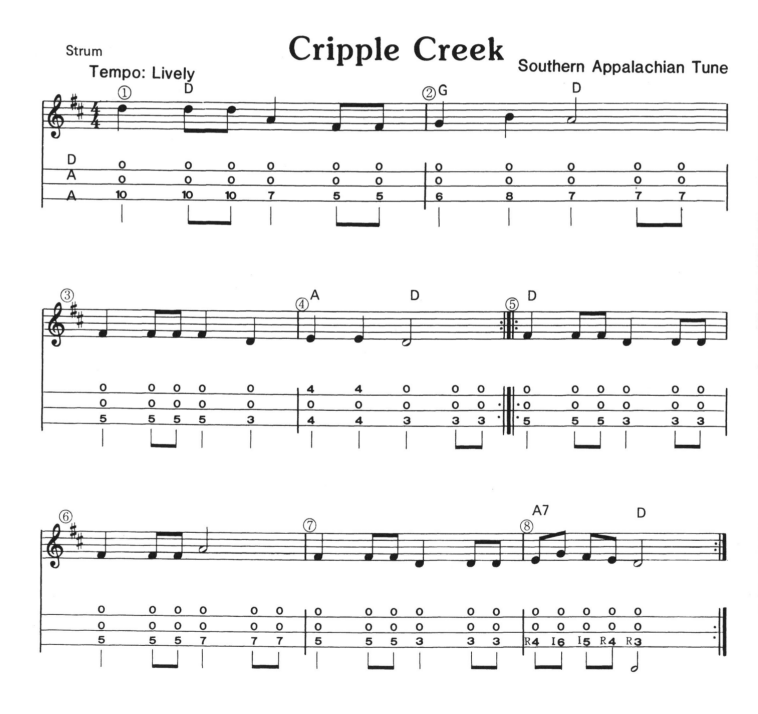

John Brown's Dream

Study all repeats first

Strum

Trad. American fiddle tune

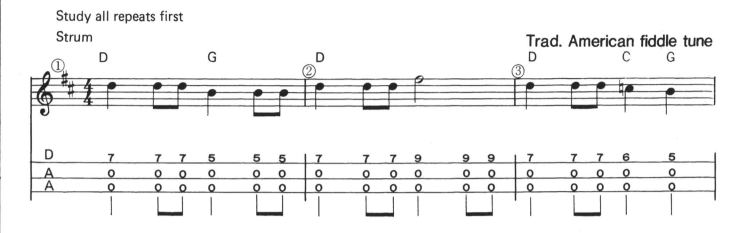

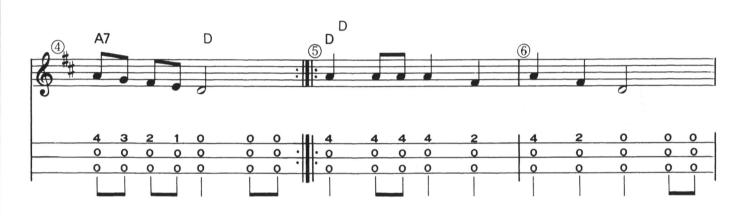

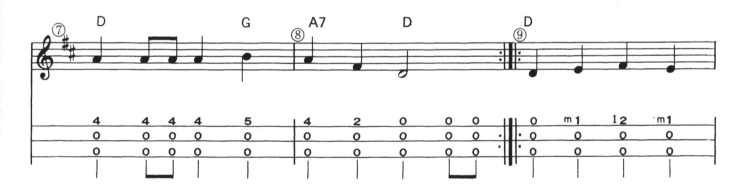

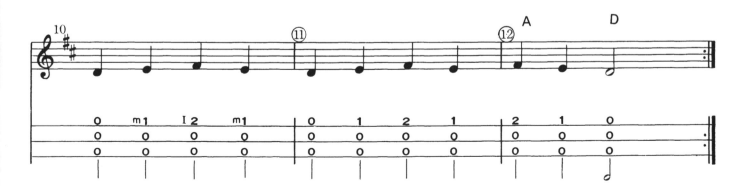

Down in the Valley

Moderate Speed

Trad. American

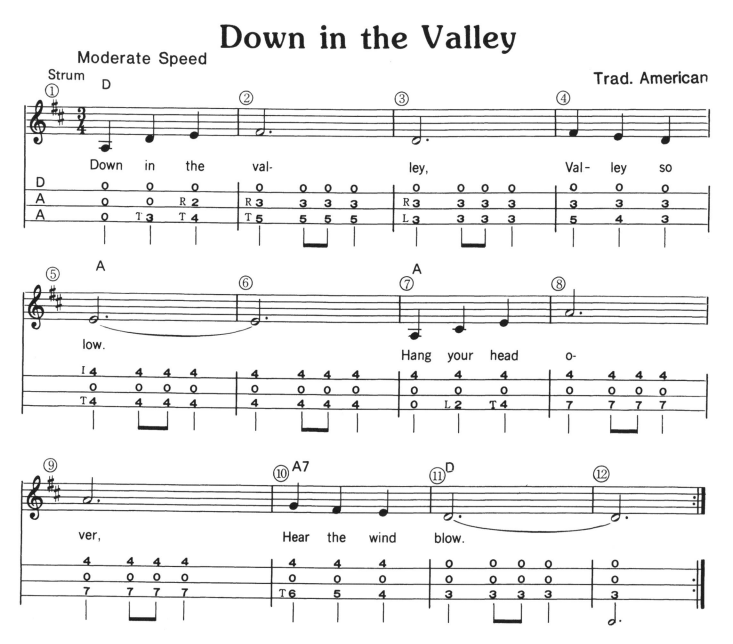

PLAYING HINTS AND INSTRUCTIONS: Notice the necessary tuning and time signature. You might wonder about counting out the dotted notes and the meaning of the curved line connecting two notes. I'm aware of your curiosity, but must ask you to wait until later. I will not forget your questions. But some very important left hand work is needed here.

Remember the stress on economy of movement in the third strumming exercise? Try the following example from DOWN IN THE VALLEY. Read each direction first, comparing it to the corresponding measure in the song before trying to play.

Measure 1 : On the 3rd beat $\begin{smallmatrix} R & 0 \\ & 2 \\ T & 4 \end{smallmatrix}$, place your little finger on the melody string, 2nd fret, <u>in addition to</u> the fingers already requested.

Measure 2 : The little finger slides to the 3rd fret melody string along with the other fingers.

Measure 3 : Now you know why. Just lifting your thumb gives you all necessary notes. Your little finger stays down through measure 4.

Measure 12 : If you're playing the song through several times, measure 12 is played $\begin{smallmatrix} 0 & 0 & 0 & 0 \\ 0 & 0 & 0 & 0 \\ 3 & 3 & 3 & 3 \end{smallmatrix}$ The last time through, you strum and hold while the sound dies away.

Down in the Valley
Harmony Part

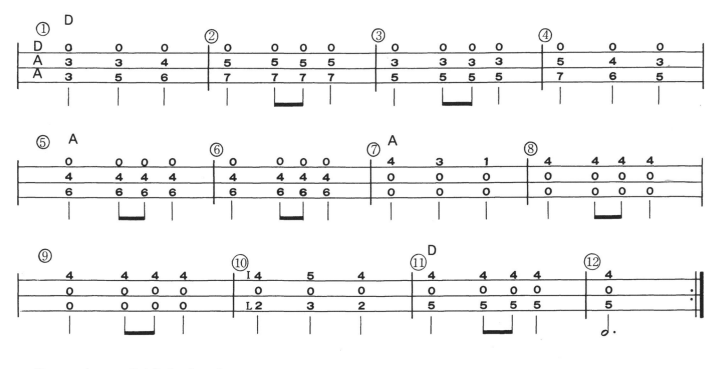

Do you have a 6 1/2 fret?   If so, you might enjoy playing the following for measure 10.

```
    4    5    6½
    0    0    0
    2    3    4
```

If you're playing through the harmony part more than once, fill out measure 12 with strums until the last time when you strum and hold.

1. Down in the valley, valley so low.
   Hang your head over, hear the wind blow.
   Hear the wind blow, dear, hear the wind blow,
   Hang your head over, hear the wind blow.

2. Roses love sunshine, violets love dew
   Angels in heaven, know I love you.
   Know I love you, dear, know I love you,
   Angels in heaven, know I love you.

3. If you don't love me, love whom you please,
   Throw your arms round me, give my heart ease.
   Give my heart ease love, give my heart ease,
   Throw your arms round me, give my heart ease.

4. Build me a castle forty feet high
   So I can see him as he rides by.
   As he rides, love, as he rides by
   So I can see him as he rides by.

5. Write me a letter, send it by mail,
   Send it in care of Birmingham jail.
   Birmingham jail love, Birmingham jail,
   Send it in care of Birmingham jail.

Ode To Joy (I)

Moderate Speed

Ludwig Van Beethoven

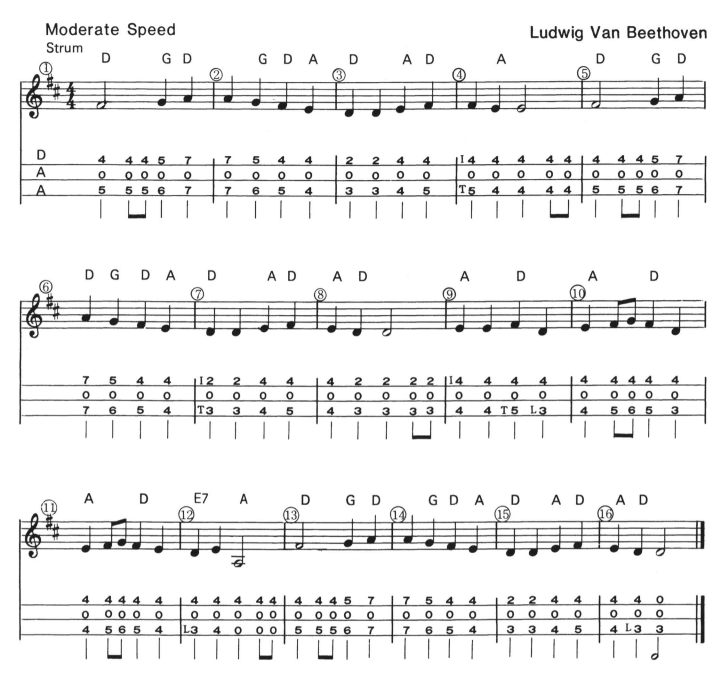

Words by Henry van Dyke

Joyful, joyful, we adore thee, God of glory, Lord of love.
Hearts unfold like flowers before thee, Opening to the sun above.
Melt the clouds of sin and sadness, Drive the dark of doubt away.
Giver of immortal gladness, Fill us with the light of day.

All thy works with joy surround thee, Earth and heaven reflect thy rays,
Stars and angels sing around thee, Center of unbroken praise.
Field and forest, vale and mountain, Flowery meadow, flashing sea,
Chanting bird and flowing fountain, Call us to rejoice in thee.

Mortals, join the happy chorus Which the morning stars began,
Father love is reigning o'er us, Brother love binds man to man.
Ever singing, march we onward, Victors in the midst of strife.
Joyful music leads us sunward In the triumph song of life.

Review

If you're lucky, the instrument has stayed in tune. If not, go through the tuning section step by step. Do not worry if the first or second or even more attempts at tuning are traumatic. Everything may still be too new. Be patient with yourself. Perhaps you've never before had to organize sounds to such a degree.

Here's a guide for a typical practice session.

1. Find the right chair and a quiet spot in which to work.
2. Place the instrument correctly on your lap and explore a few plucked sounds.
3. Now is the time to learn fret numbers. Study the landmarks of the 3rd, 6th and 10th frets. Close you eyes, envision a fret number—4, for example—open your eyes and go for it. Don't let yourself count 1, 2, 3,4. Use the 3rd fret landmark and head for the next fret. You can complicate this exercise by envisioning a particular string also, say 5th fret, bass string. You'll be surprised how quickly you can skip this part of your practice sessions. Don't take the "easy" way out by putting masking tape or something else with numbers written on it by the frets. Go cold turkey and get this part of your learning out of the way within the first week.
4. Strumming will probably take longer than learning fret numbers. Correctly approached, this skill soon becomes automatic so you can concentrate on your left hand which has more complex work. Refer to the strumming section of the book and go through each strumming situation—first through the air and then over the strings. Please give this practice area enough time, energy and concentration.
5. Just using your left hand, move through parts of a tune or random notes. Make sure you slide over the strings. Make the movements definite.

Oh, Susanna

Moderately fast

Stephen Foster

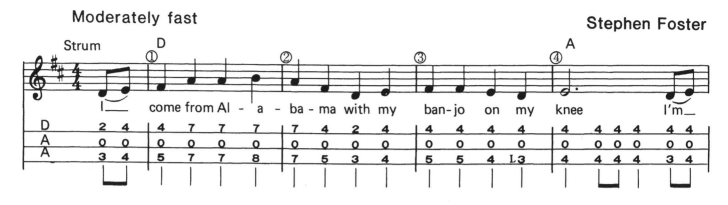

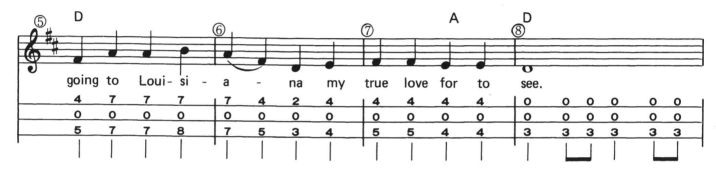

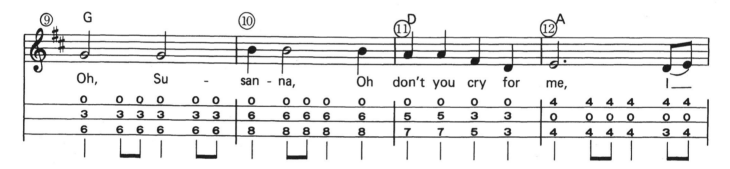

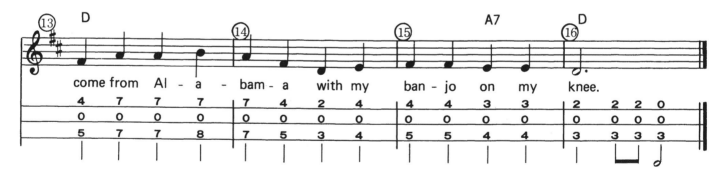

Practice Hint: In the 3rd chord of measure 11, put your little finger down at the 3rd fret in addition to the thumb at the 5th fret. To get to the next chord, you simply lift your thumb. Remember, it's easier to get notes by lifting fingers than by putting them down.

It rained all night the day I left, the weather it was dry, The sun so hot I froze to death, Susanna don't you cry. Oh, Susanna, oh don't you cry for me, I come from Alabama with my banjo on my knee.

Lesson 2: Chord Study and Other Left Hand Work

We'll focus on the left hand.

Place your thumb at the 5th fret melody string and your index finger at the 4th fret bass string. Look at your hand. It should be curved with fingers dropped comfortably on the fretboard. Fingers not currently in use should be ready to play (in other words, not tucked under the palm or flying in the air). Move your hand off the fretboard for a moment and let's talk. Do you have long fingernails? If so, how partial to them are you? Very short fingernails on the left hand are practically essential to comfortable, assertive playing. Long nails mean your left hand will flatten out on the strings rather than be curved. Conversely, sturdy nails on the right hand are a good help with volume and contrast when you fingerpick. Classical guitarists often go through life with longish, blunt-cut nails on the right hand and clipped, short nails on the left hand.

Back to the fretboard. Place your thumb at the 5th fret melody string, index finger at the 4th fret bass string. Again, curve your hand.

Throughout this exercise your index finger remains stationary at the 4th fret. Your thumb moves to the 4th fret, back to the 5th fret, to the 6th fret, to the 7th fret (if it reaches), back to the 6th, 5th and 4th frets. Now, as you lift your thumb, place your little finger on the 3rd fret (remember fluid movement), move it to the 2nd fret and then back to the 3rd fret. Written in tablature, it looks like this:

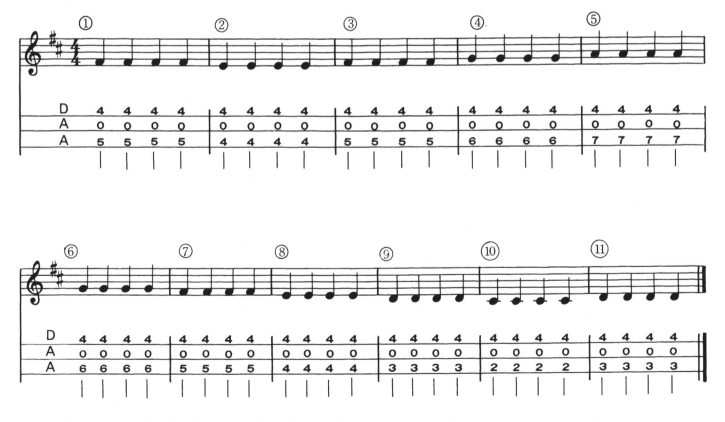

You can practice the above exercise using any four-beat strumming pattern on each chord.

31

THREE FINGER CHORDS

During a later lesson we'll discuss chords in some depth. But since they sound so lovely on the dulcimer, we'll work with them by discussing shapes first. Four shapes produce many chords in the DAA tuning. We'll study them one by one and then put them together in some tunes.

SHAPE I 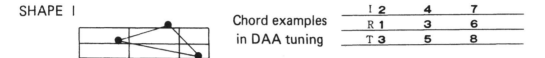 Chord examples
in DAA tuning

I	2	4	7
R	1	3	6
T	3	5	8

Form the chord first. Relax your hand. Practice lifting your hand and putting it down - all three fingers at once. When the shape feels comfortable, move to the next shape.

SHAPE II Chord examples
in DAA tuning

I	3	4	7	10
L	1	2	5	8
T	3	4	7	10

EXERCISE USING SHAPES I AND II

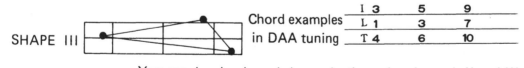

IMPORTANT: Think of your fingers as musical spiders walking about! Work on the choreography of your finger movements through the exercise. Fingers which are common to the next chord ($\frac{4}{3}$ to $\frac{4}{2}$ for example) should remain stationary. Ultimately the
idea is to play without looking so much at the fretboard. Feeling your way along certainly helps.

SHAPE III   Chord examples
in DAA tuning

I	3	5	9
L	1	3	7
T	4	6	10

You can do a lovely scale hamonization using shapes I, II and III.

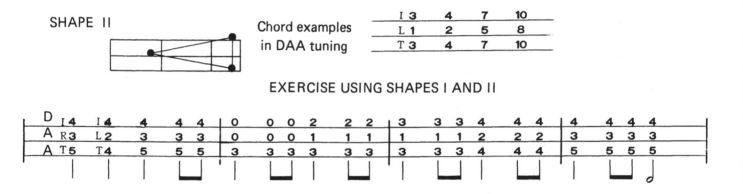

		D	E	F♯	G	A	B	C♯	D
D	0	I 4	I 4	I 5	I 7	I 7	I 8	I 9	
A	0	L 2	R 3	L 3	L 5	R 6	R 7	L 7	
A	3	T 4	T 5	T 6	T 7	T 8	T 9	T 10	

SHAPE IV: The barre chord.

m 4	L 4
R 4	L 4
L 4	L 4

1st fingering   2nd fingering

There are two handy fingerings for this chord:

I usually use the first fingering, mostly out of familiarity. Following is an exercise
for the barre chord using the first fingering.

Place a barre at the 4th fret. Leaving all fingers down, place your thumb at the
5th fret, move to the 6th fret, back to the 5th fret, then lift your thumb.

$\frac{3}{4}$ Time

D	4	4	4	4	4	4	4	4	4	4	4	4	4	4	4	4	4	4	4
A	4	4	4	4	4	4	4	4	4	4	4	4	4	4	4	4	4	4	4
A	4	4	4	4	5	5	5	5	6	6	6	6	5	5	5	5	4	4	4	4

If you use the first fingering, be sure to leave your little finger at the 4th fret while
You play other tones with your thumb.

I've been asked why I use a L-R-M fingering on a barre chord rather than a R-M-I fingering
which seems easier. The L-R-M fingering frees my index finger for bass string work in
addition to having the thumb available.

As you continue to play, your tones will become more clear and you'll instinctively
know how hard to press to get musical tones. If you play a chord and some notes seem more
like thumps, ask yourself these questions:

1.   Am I pressing hard enough?

2.   Am I pulling any of the strings rather than pressing down?

3.   Are any of my fingers on top of the frets?

4.   Am I strumming evenly and freely across the strings?

Ode to Joy II

This version of ODE TO JOY has more chords and you might enjoy it more than version I. I feel, however, that the best version is yet to come, so I encourage you to try this one for academic practice in the movement of three finger chords.

DOTTED NOTES: The most important new skill to work with in this arrangement is handling dotted notes. Again, the mathematicians were the greatest influence on the organization of musical sounds, and that is evident once more with dotted notes. Suppose a composer wants to hold a note just a little longer, but not as long as another beat. A dot following a note does the trick. The dot is worth 50% of the note it follows.

THE FOLLOWING 2 EXAMPLES ASSUME THE TIME SIGNATURE AT THE BEGINNING OF THE MUSIC IS 4/4

A half note is worth 2 beats. The dot, therefore, is worth 1 beat. The dotted half note is then worth 3 beats. 𝅗𝅥.

A quarter note is worth 1 beat. The dot, therefore, is worth ½ beat. The dotted quarter note is then worth 1½ beats. ♩.

CHANGE THE TIME SIGNATURE TO 6/8.

An eighth note is worth 1 beat. The dot, therefore, is worth ½ beat. The dotted eighth note is then worth 1½ beats. ♪.

Most of the time the next note reflects the remainder of the beat. For example, a dotted quarter note ♩. worth 1½ beats is usually followed by an eighth note (♪) worth ½ beat. That "clears the slate" and the rhythm can continue.

Understanding dots is one thing; playing them is another. A wonderful musician and friend, Lorraine Lee, suggested to me that a beginning player can keep the pick moving in the air to help keep time. For example: The following two chords have a combined value of 2 beats—the first chord is worth 1½ beats; the second, ½ beat. Look at them with everything divided into ½ beats.

Unstrummed ½ beats

Practice the following measure which has easier chords.

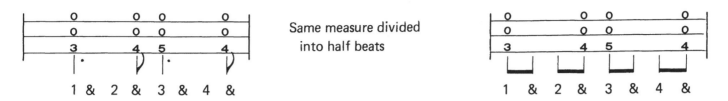

Same measure divided
into half beats

Actually strum where you see bold arrows. Strum in the air where you see broken arrows.

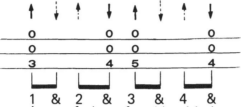

It will probably take you some time to feel comfortable with dotted notes. Sometimes
an extra strum is written in the accompaniment. This helps with the counting,
but may still need practice for the coordination. Refer to ODE TO JOY below, measures 4, 8 and 16.

Ode To Joy (II)

35

Au clair de la lune

"Au Clair de la Lune" was written by Jean Baptiste Lully, a composer at the court of Louis XIV and is one of the most popular folk songs of France. The tempo is moderate. Most of the song is played with the thumb and index finger. This tune is practice for the barre chord.

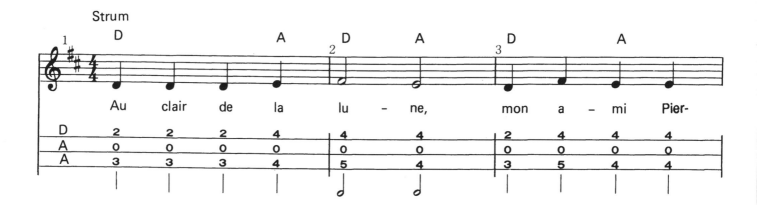

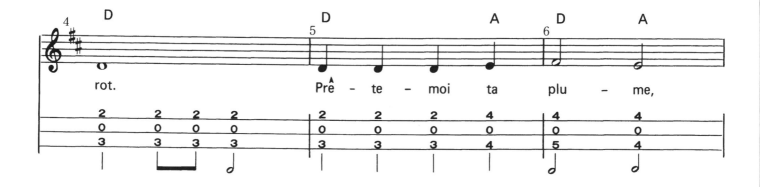

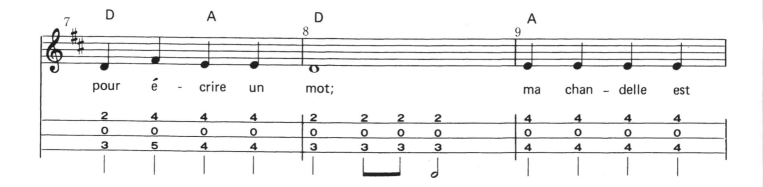

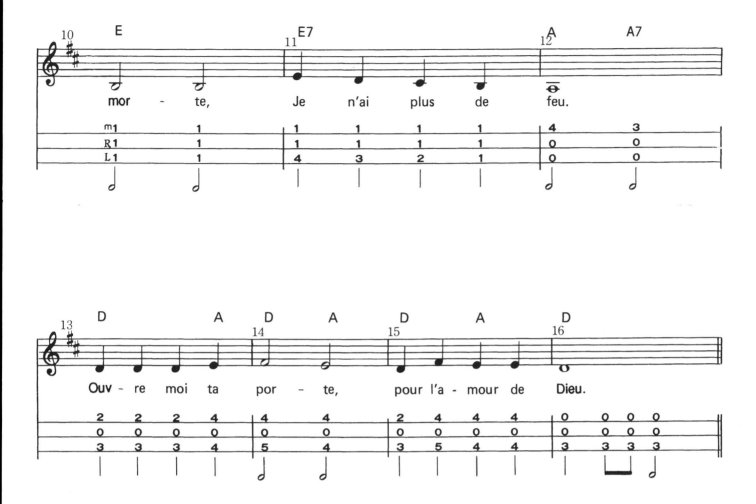

Playing suggestions: Measures 10 and 11 will probably present the most problems. Practice measure 10 by placing the fingers indicated on the strings at the 1st fret, picking them up and placing them again as smoothly as possible. In measure 11, leave your little finger on the melody string when you place your thumb at the 4th fret. You now have two fingers on one string - but only the tone closest to the bridge will sound. Move your thumb to the 3rd fret and then the 2nd. Now, as you return to the 1st fret you only pick up your thumb rather than pick up your thumb while putting down your little finger again. You have cut the playing action by 50%. Begin to get into the habit of leaving fingers down when you can. This helps with stability and sometimes permits you to move more quickly.

Flop-Eared Mule

Playing hints for Flop-Earned Mule

1. Music has form and design that works around phrases and repeats. As you play more music—especially fiddle tunes—you'll find most tunes have one section (called "A") which is played and repeated, followed by another section (called "B") which is played and repeated. The form of these tunes is A A B B. Flop-Eared Mule has a different form—A A B A A. I've also heard it played A A B B A A.
2. Fingering is important. Please follow my suggestions—or make sure any variations of yours will really work when the tune is played fast.
3. You must slide in measure 4. Do not "walk" your fingers.
4. Much of the B part works off a barre chord at the 4th fret.
5. Measure 12 is probably the most difficult in the piece. It could prevent you from playing fast. Spend extra time working out this measure.

Flop - Eared Mule

Play: A A B A A

Traditional American
Arr. Lorraine Lee
Adapted: Madeline MacNeil

Golden Slippers

Traditional Tune

You'll be learning about chords and their uses later. But I want to introduce you to the A chord, the root of which (the A) is found at the 4th fret of the bass string. You can play off the A chord by putting your index finger at the 4th fret bass; using your little finger to play notes found at the 2nd and 3rd frets, melody string; and using your thumb for notes at the 4th, 5th, 6th and 7th frets, melody. Practice this by doing exactly that. Put your index finger at the 4th fret, bass string, and play from the 2nd fret to the 7th (if you can reach that far) and back to the 2nd.

Following the same method, you can work off a G chord, the root of which is found at the 3rd fret, bass string.

Don't forget the repeat of the first eight measures in this tune.

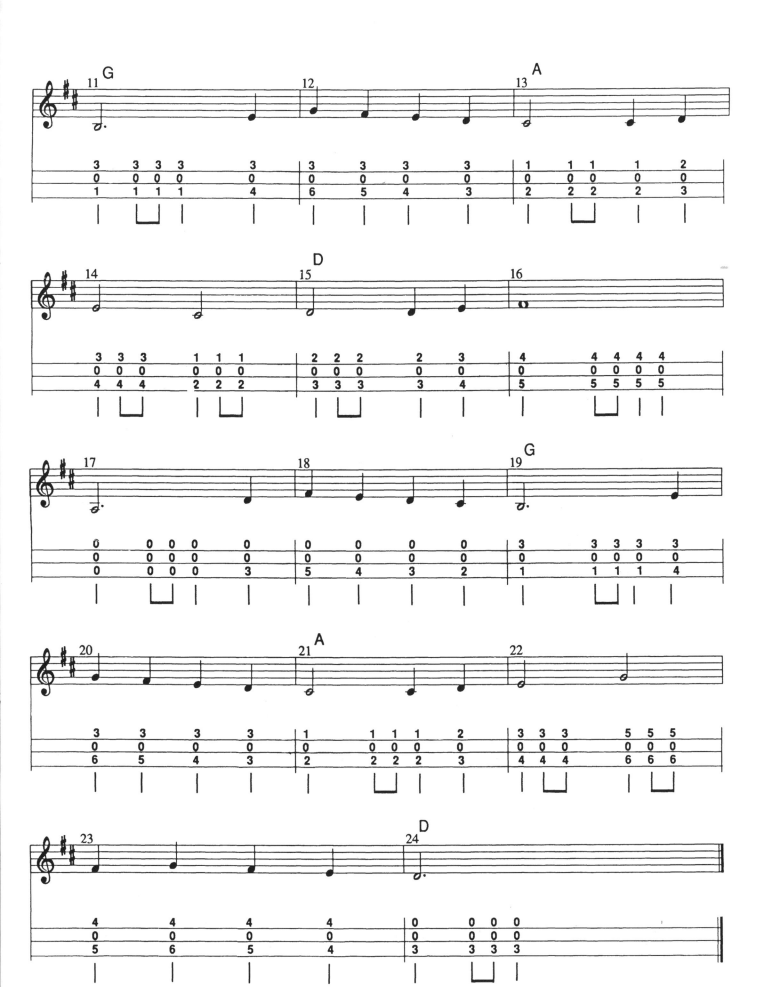

Lesson 3: Picking and Strumming,
Fingerstyle Playing

You probably noticed that the music chosen to illustrate heavily chorded music moved slowly or moderately so. If the left hand is forming many chords, it's rather difficult to move fast. But some music calls for this texture - hymns especially. The time has come to combine chords and individual notes for a lighter texture.

The tablature looks just the same, but you'll find individual notes amid the chords.

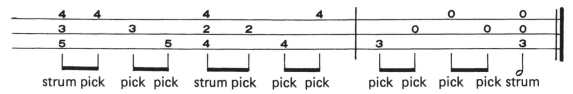

Try this technique on the third version of Ode To Joy. If necessary, review the directions for playing dotted notes.

Ode To Joy (III)

Fingerpicking

You can produce lovely sounds by using right hand fingers and fingernails against the strings. I know fine players who use finger and thumb picks for volume, but I've never had success with such implements. There is something special in the contact of finger against string.

To begin, place your right hand thumb on the melody string, index finger on the middle string and middle finger on the bass string. Do not anchor your little finger on the instrument or the bridge.

Pluck each string, one by one, until the sound is fairly smooth. This is three - finger picking.

Double - thumbing means the right hand thumb covers the melody and middle strings while the index finger works with the bass string. Give double - thumbing a try on a sequence like melody, bass, middle, bass and back to the melody string. I use both techniques and enjoy them both.

Three-finger picking or double - thumbing would be appropriate for the following song.

Simple Gifts

This Shaker song dates back to approximately 1848.   The Shakers enjoyed their "gift to be simple" and this was reflected in their songs, which did not avoid lively tunes.   "Simple Gifts" is an integral part of APPALACHIAN SPRING, a ballet choreographed by Martha Graham with music by Aaron Copeland.

Measure 1: You can play chords either by brushing across the strings with any right-hand finger or by plucking all three strings at once.

Measure 3: Obviously you'll have to pluck the strings to get two note chords. You simply form the chord with your left hand and, with your right hand, pluck (at the same time) whatever strings are requested. In this case that would be the bass and melody strings.

Remember your math. If a note is worth three beats, you can easily break your picking rhythm into quarter notes, eighth notes, or a combination; but everything must add up to three beats. Consider fingerpicking when arranging tunes and songs. Generally, tunes played in a slow to moderate tempo are better candidates for fingerpicking, especially when you are new at this method.

Arrangements are up to you. Please feel free to change my arrangements in any way you wish as you develop your playing skills. I play the tunes differently each time I approach them, sometimes foregoing a pick for fingers or vice versa. Those of us who arrange tunes are simply giving you suggestions.

Amazing Grace

Fingerpicking makes a nice background for "Amazing Grace", but first we have important practice work with the left hand.

The goal is smooth playing and this means thinking ahead. ALWAYS think ahead and plan your moves.

Isolate measures 1 and 2.

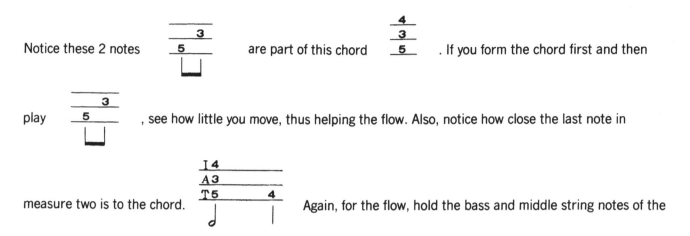

Notice these 2 notes ⟨tab: 3 / 5⟩ are part of this chord ⟨tab: 4 / 3 / 5⟩ . If you form the chord first and then

play ⟨tab: 3 / 5⟩ , see how little you move, thus helping the flow. Also, notice how close the last note in

measure two is to the chord. ⟨tab: I4 / A3 / T5 4⟩ Again, for the flow, hold the bass and middle string notes of the

chord while you slide your thumb to the 4th fret.

Isolate measures 7 and 8. See how easily most of the two measures can be played off a barre chord at the 4th fret.

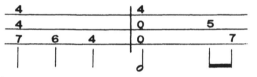

To make everything sound nice, again study measures 7 and 8. To determine which notes are accompaniments

to other notes. The melody and the word "me" are taken care of by the ⟨tab: 4 / 4 / 7⟩ chord. Notes, until you reach

the word "I", are accompanying or embellishing and should be played lighter—with the exception of the ⟨tab: 4 / 0 / 0⟩

chord which begins a measure. That needs more stress. So much to think about, but all these little things go together to make music.

General Rule: When playing music like "Amazing Grace" with a combination of picking and strumming, notice notes in each chord (or nearby notes) which are played before or after the chord. Then try to combine the chords and those notes.

Look at measures 3 and 11 for a handy fingering technique that will take some time to develop. The little finger can cover two frets at once, freeing other fingers for other work. This fingering is to be used on the

chord ⟨tab: 3 / 1 / 1⟩ . You probably won't get much sound at first and your little finger might hurt a little. But please

continue to work on this fingering as it is very useful.

Amazing Grace

Words by John Newton 1725- 1807

Amazing grace, how sweet the sound
That saved a wretch like me.
I once was lost, but now am found
Was blind, but now I see.

'Twas grace that taught my heart to fear,
And grace my fears relieved;
How precious did that grace appear
The hour I first believed.

Through many dangers, toils and snares,
I have already come;
'Tis grace hath brought me safe thus far,
And grace will lead me home.

The Lord has promised good to me,
His word my hope secures.
He will my shield and portion be
As long as life endures.

Lesson 4: Exploring Chords

If you play another instrument such as the guitar, perhaps chords are not mysteries. But, if you've formerly been afraid of them, relax. First, we'll try to understand chord construction. Since we're tuned DAA right now, we'll work with the D scale. Yes, I meant to say D scale since chords need scale notes for basic construction. Since some of you may not be familiar with musical notation, I'll be sure to name each note for you now. Notes in the D scale are:

(on your dulcimer in its current tuning, these notes can be found on the melody and middle strings, frets 3 - 10).

A chord consists of three or more notes. When you start at any degree of the scale you then use every other note in the scale for the chord. For example, a D chord is D, F#, A.

a G chord is G,B,D.

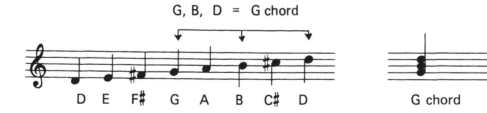

an A chord is A,C#,E.

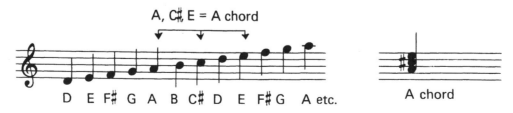

46

You might be interested to know this: number each degree of the scale (forget fret numbers for a moment).

D	E	F♯	G	A	B	C♯	D
1	2	3	4	5	6	7	1

Does it make sense to call a chord built on the first degree of the scale (in this case, D) a 1 chord? Or one built on the 4th degree a 4 chord? Musicians do, as those numbers (generic, in a sense) can be trans-- ferred to other scales. However, Roman numerals are used rather than Arabic ones.

Chord theory is such an interesting subject and we can only flirt with it here. If a sample intrigues you, I encourage you to look for books on chord theory in your local library. They'll assume you know musical notation though, so you may have to work on that first.

The D scale forms seven unaltered chords, four of which are more prevalent in most folk tunes. Some of the unaltered chords are widely used in a tune; others are generally used for "spice". In the listing below, the chords appear according to their typical frequency in a tune,

1st	D chord D F# A (I chord)	5th-7th
2nd	A chord A C# E (V chord)	E minor chord E G B (II chord)
3rd	G chord G B D (IV chord)	F# minor chord F# A C# (III chord)
4th	B minor chord B D F# (VI chord)	C# diminished chord C# E G (VII chord)

You probably have some questions and I'll anticipate some you might have.

1. **What is a minor chord?** A reading of the section on retuning will explain half steps. There are seven half steps between the first and last tones of a regular triad (chord). In a D major chord, (D F♯ A), there are four half steps between the D and the F♯ and three half steps between the F♯ and the A. When the chord is a major chord with that spacing between tones, the major statis is assumed and the chord is just written D (or whatever). Anything other than that must be labeled.

   A D minor chord (D F A) has three half steps between the first two notes (D-F) and four half tones between the last two notes (F-A). Chords (major, minor, etc.) are determined by the number of internal half steps.

2. **I've seen chords with 7's after them (A⁷ for example) in some song books. What does that mean?** A chord with a7 after it requires four tones instead of three. The same formula applies: every other note in the scale. A7 would be A, C♯, E, G. You can also find notes with 9's, 11's, 13's and so forth after them (although mainly in jazz and modern classical music). Same rules apply.

3. **You mention a C♯ Diminished chord as the VII chord based on the D scale. What is a diminished chord?** I was afraid you'd ask about that. We're just touching the tip of the iceberg as far as chord theory goes. After all, this is a book concerning playing the dulcimer. If you delve into chord theory you'll find all kinds of interesting variations. A diminished chord has one less half step within the chord. There are three half steps between the first and second tones of the diminished chord (in this case C♯ and E) and three half steps between the second and third tones of the chord (in this case, between the E and the G).

4. **I've seen E minor chords, E min chords, and Em chords. Are they all the same?** Yes.

Tuned as we are (D A A), D chords abound on the dulcimer. If we follow exceptions which say tones can be doubled (Ex. D F♯ A D), left out (ex. D A A), and played out of order (ex. F♯ D A), there are even more possibilities.

Notes on the fretboard in D A A Tuning

Tuning : D A A

D	E	F♯	G	A	B	C	C♯	D	E	F♯	G	
A	B	C♯	D	E	F♯	G	G♯	A	B	C♯	D	etc.
A	B	C♯	D	E	F♯	G	G♯	A	B	G♯	D	

Fret Numbers Open   1   2   3   4   5   6   6 1/2   7   8   9   10

See where you could find some D chords? Some A chords? Here are some chords in tablature. The small letters following fret numbers tell which notes you are actually playing. See how the chord notes are juggled? Can you hear the difference in musical sound between the first two A chord examples? One secret to creative playing is knowing when to use what form of a chord to obtain the sound you want. Experiment!

D Chords

0 D	2 F♯	0 D	4 A	4 A	7 D	7 D	9 F♯
0 A	0 A	0 A	0 A	3 D	5 F♯	0 A	7 A
0 D	3 D	5 F♯	5 F♯	5 F♯	7 A	7 A	10 D

G chords

3 G	5 B	7 D
1 B	3 D	6 G
3 D	6 G	8 B

A chords

4 A	4 A	4 A	4 A
0 A	2 C♯	4 E	4 E
4 E	4 E	4 E	7 A

A7 Chords

3 G	4 A
0 A	4 E
4 E	6 G

B minor chords

2 F♯	5 B	7 D
1 B	3 D	5 F♯
3 D	5 F♯	8 B

Practice these chords and, when they feel comfortable, memorize a few. Now return to earlier lessons in the book. Most tunes have chord markings over the musical notation. You and a friend can play the tunes and chord accompaniments together.

The doors to music begin to open; now to open them further.

Suppose you see a familiar tune in a loved song book and would like to try singing it while chording. But the key signature looks different. For example, you see G chords and even a C chord. You have probably encountered something in the key of G. Your first thought might be to turn the page and look for something in D. But you *can* accompany most of the tunes in G. The only chord you haven't played is C. The G scale is as follows:

Key Signature for key of G

G   A   B   C   D   E   F♯   G

The I chord is G – (G B D)

The V chord is D –(D F♯A)

The IV chord is C – (C E G)

The VI chord is E minor (E G B)

A good C chord is $\underline{6}$
$$\underline{4}$$
$$\underline{6}$$

In fact, you don't have many choices. The only C's to be found in this tuning are on the bass string at the 6th and 13th frets.

The following songs—"Home on the Range," "She'll Be Coming 'Round the Mountain" and "When Johnny Comes Marching Home"—are to be accompanied with chords and sung. If you want to play the melody of the tunes, refer to the section on playing with a capo where you'll find tablature for them.

She'll be Coming 'Round the Mountain

She'll be com - ing round the moun - tain when she comes. She'll be

com - ing round the moun - tain when she comes. She'll be

com - ing round the moun - tain, She'll be com - ing round the moun - tain, She'll be

com - ing round the moun - tain when she comes.

2. She'll be driving six white horses when she comes.
3. Oh, we'll all go out to meet her when she comes.
4. She'll wear the red pajamas when she comes.
5. She'll have to sleep with Grandma when she comes.
6. Oh, we'll kill the old red rooster when she comes.
7. We'll have chicken pie and dumplings when she comes.

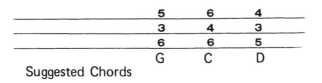

Suggested Chords

Home on the Range

Suggested Chords   G   C   A7   D   D7

Suggested Strumming pattern

Oh, give me the land where the bright diamond sand
Throws its light from the glittering streams,
Where glideth along the graceful white swan,
Like the maid to her heavenly dreams.

How often at night, when the heavens were bright,
With the light of the twinkling stars,
Have I stood here amazed and asked as I gazed
If their glory exceeds that of ours.

The air is so pure and the breezes so free,
The zephyrs so balmy and light,
That I would not exchange my home here to range
Forever in azures so bright.

When Johnny Comes Marching Home

When John-ny comes march-ing home a-gain, hu-rah, _____ hu-rah, _____ We'll give him a hear-ty wel-come then, hu-rah, _____ hu-rah. _____ The men will cheer and the boys will shout, the la-dies they will all turn out, and we'll all feel gay when John-ny comes march-ing home. _____

You could easily pass "When Johnny comes Marching Home Again" by, thinking it would be impossible to accompany. Yet, with nimble fingers and a few extra chords, you can play it. Give it a try. The chords you need are below.

The song is in the key of E minor – a key that shares the same key signature as G major.

The old church bell will peal with joy, hurah, hurah,
To welcome home our darling boy, hurah, hurah,
The village lads and lassies say,
With roses they will strew the way,
And we'll all feel gay when Johnny comes marching home.

Get ready for the jubilee, hurah, hurah,
We'll give the hero three times three, hurah, hurah,
The laurel wreath is ready now
To place upon his loyal brow,
And we'll all feel gay when Johnny comes marching home.

Let love and friendship on that day, hurah, hurah,
Their choicest treasures then display, hurah, hurah,
And let each one perform some part,
To fill with joy the warrior's heart,
And we'll all feel gay when Johnny comes marching home.

Suggested Chords

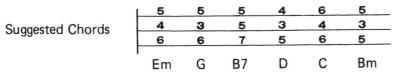

	5	5	5	4	6	5
	4	3	5	3	4	3
	6	6	7	5	6	5
	Em	G	B7	D	C	Bm

Question: I thought tied notes only connected notes from one measure to the next.

Answer: They also create notes of perhaps a strange value. In measure 7, for example, the tied notes are worth 5 beats (refer to time signature) and a note worth 3 beats tied to a note worth 2 beats is the most efficient way to indicate 5 beats.

I chose "She'll be Coming Round the Mountain", "Home on the Range", and "When Johnny Comes Marching Home" on purpose. Each one has a different character and could be enhanced by different accompaniments - each of them easy.

"She'll be Coming Round the Mountain" needs a crisp rhythmic strum. If yours is rather mushy, mark in strum directions and work them out.

"Home on the Range" moves slower. Perhaps a finger-picked broken chord accompaniment would be nice. What is a broken chord? Here are some definitions:

Chord: The notes of a chord are played all at once. $\frac{4}{2}$ 4

(strum)

Arpeggio: The notes of a chord are played one at a time in order – low to high.

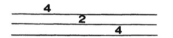

Broken Chord: The notes of a chord are played in a pattern or in random order.

"When Johnny Comes Marching Home" leads the imagination to a drum–roll or military feeling. To capture this feeling, strum sparsely with authority and sing over the notes which are dying away. For example:

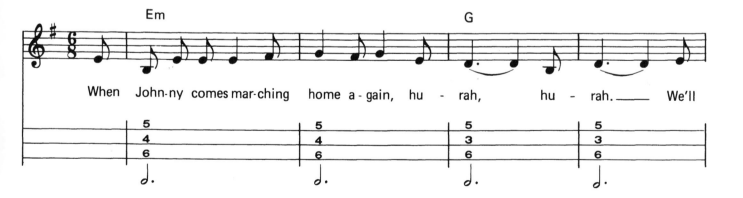

Lesson 5

Singing While You Play

Please consider your voice the fine instrument it is by allowing it room to work. Sit up straight when you play and sing, being sure to look up from the dulcimer at least occasionally.

Back-Up Playing

You should consider singing song after song, accompanying with chords. I couldn't begin to write out dozens of appropriate songs, but instead will list some and include the typical chords used to accompany them. The following songs begin with the D chord except where noted.

Blowing in the Wind	D G Bmin A
500 Miles	D G Bmin A
Today (While the Blossoms Still Cling to the Vine)	D G Bmin A
America	D A Bmin G
America the Beautiful	D A E G Bmin
You Are My Sunshine	D G A
Irene, Good Night, Irene	D A G
Go Tell Aunt Rody	D A
Happy Birthday to You	D A A⁷ G
Darlin' Clementine	D A
My Bonnie Lies Over the Ocean	D G E A A⁷
When the Saints Go Marching In	D A G
He's Got the Whole World in His Hand	D A G
Swing Low, Sweet Chariot	D A G
We Wish You a Merry Christmas	D A A⁷ G E
I've Been Working on the Railroad (Begins with G chord)	G C A⁷ D
Kum Ba Yah	D A G

. . . plus all the songs written out in this book and dozens more.

Things to try: After you feel comfortable with the chord structure of a song, be adventuresome and move fingers around while you hold a chord. Does knowing the chord structure help you pick out the melody?

Away in a Manger

The arrangement of "Away in a Manger" has several possibilities. First and foremost, it is a suggestion of how to arrange songs for singing. Most players get tired of continually playing the same notes they're singing and want ideas for variety. Following are some suggestions.

1. Use an introduction and have it set the mood of the song.
2. Remember the bass string—nice notes lie there.
3. When playing a slower song, work for sustain by holding down notes of a chord while you're singing and/or playing individual notes. Listen for the sustained notes and sing with them.

Ways to play and sing "Away in a Manger":

I chose this song not only because it is beautiful, but because it is well known. Make sure you know a song well before working on accompaniments. Try the song with Accompaniment I. A friend can add in Accompaniment II. Working on your own, try playing Accompaniment II while singing the melody. In case you want to try this as an instrumental trio, there is tablature for the melody.

Away in a Manger
Accompaniment I

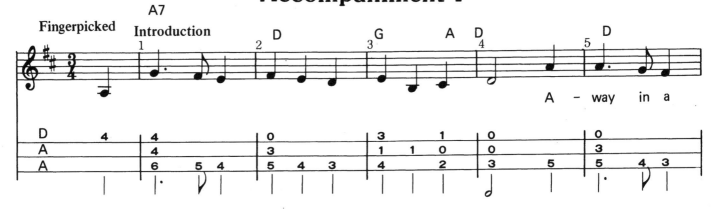

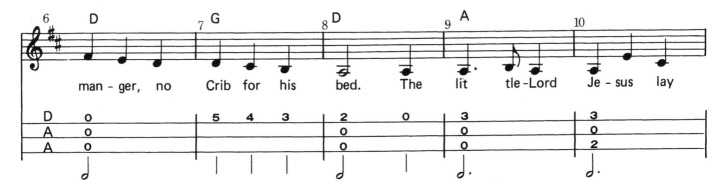

The cattle are lowing, the baby awakes,
But little Lord Jesus, no crying he makes,
I love thee, Lord Jesus, look down from the sky,
And stay by my cradle till morning is nigh.

Be near me, Lord Jesus, I ask thee to stay,
Close by me forever, and love me, I pray.
Bless all the dear children in thy tender care,
And fit us for heaven to live with thee there.

Away in a Manger
Accompaniment II

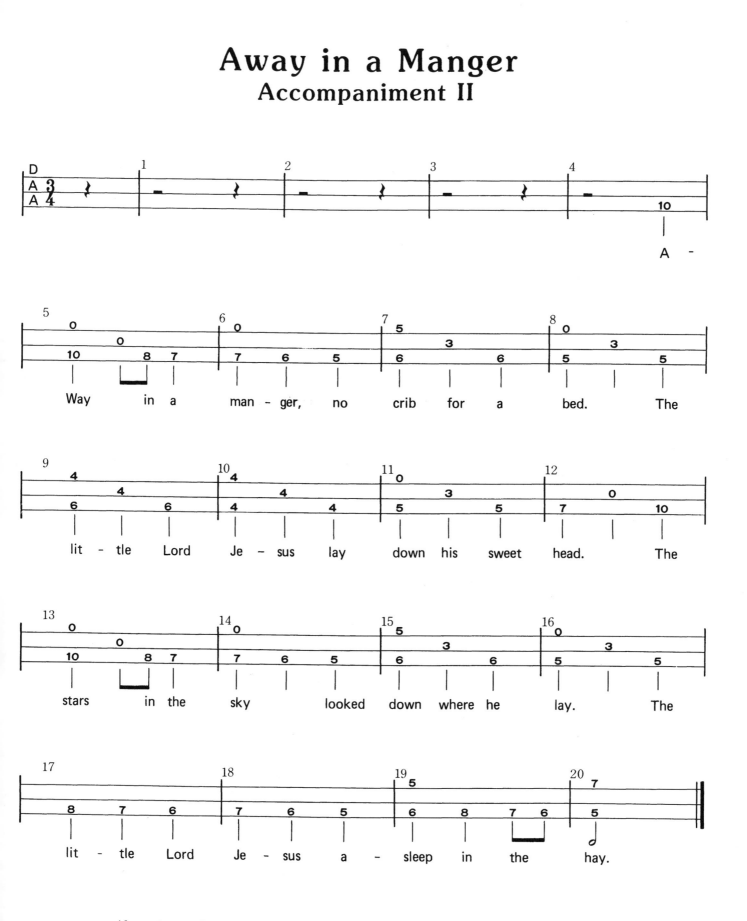

If you have a 6 ½ fret, play measure 19:

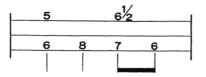

Away in a Manger
Melody

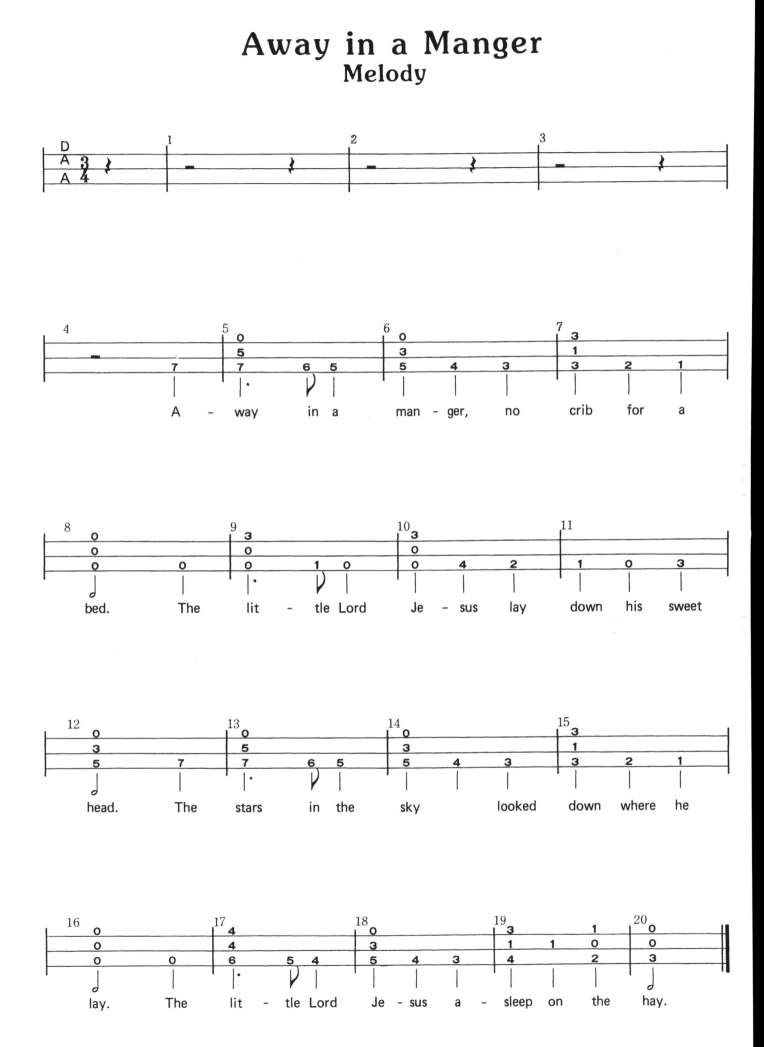

The Ash Grove

Melody

Traditional Welsh

You can consider playing this beautiful melody a review of the pick-strum techniques used with "Simple Gifts."
Play lightly; let the notes ring.

The Ash Grove

If you enjoy singing, use the harmony as an accommpaniment for your voice. The words are haunting and lovely.

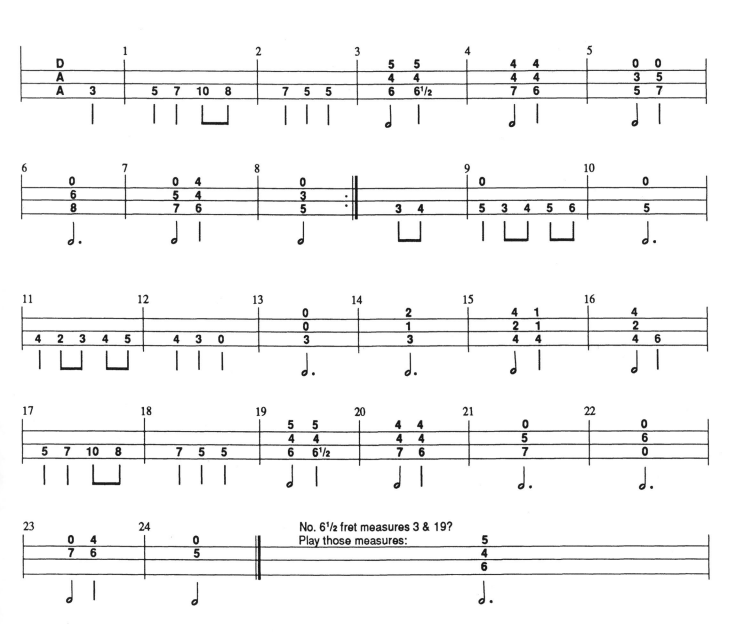

The ash grove how graceful, how plainly 'tis speaking
The harp through it playing has language for me.
Whenever the light through its branches is breaking,
A host of kind faces is gazing on me.
The friends of my childhood again are before me;
Each step wakes a memory as freely I roam.
With soft whispers laden, its leaves rustle o'er me,
The ash grove, the ash grove alone is my home.

My laughter is over, my step loses lightness,
Old countryside measures steal soft on my ear.
I only remember the past and its brightness;
The dear ones I mourn for again gather here.
From out of the shadows their loving looks greet me.
And wistfully searching the leafy green dome,
I find other faces fond bending to greet me.
The ash grove, the ash grove alone is my home.

Arkansas Traveler

Trad. American Tune

Always check the tuning directions for the dulcimer found at the beginning of the tablatures throughout the book.

This wonderful fiddle tune is a great practice for light, dancing playing. Remember: <u>No thumb</u> on "Arkansas Traveler," as you play only on the melody string.

62A

Lesson 6

Tuning, Retuning, and Why

DEFINITION: Interval . . . the distance between one musical note and another.

We've worked in one tuning and perhaps you wonder why we've usually played only in the key of D. I chose the key of D for this book because it is compatible with most dulcimers. Now, why must you eventually tune differently? Look at your fretboard. See the wide spaces between some frets while other spaces have evenly spaced frets. Your dulcimer skips some notes, and therefore, is a DIATONIC instrument rather than CHROMATIC.

Definitions

DIATONIC: An adjective applied to scales using combinations of whole steps and half steps.
CHROMATIC: An adjective applied to a scale which includes 12 half steps in an octave.

Music in the Western Hemisphere is based on an interval of one half step. If music of Japan, China, India and some other countries sound somewhat out of tune to your ears, it's because the basic interval is less than one half step . . . a quarter step, for example. The best place to see half steps laid out for you is a piano. Move from any piano key to the nearest piano key (be it black or white) and you've moved a half-step.

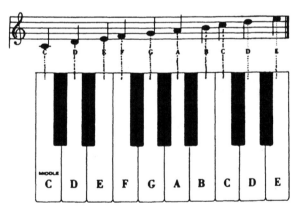

Look at the illustration of a piano keyboard section. Find middle C. Beginning with middle C, count the number of half steps to C' (the octave above). I hope you found 12. If not, count again. Count the number of half steps between D and D'. Still 12. This twelve tone scale is chromatic. Look at the keyboard section again and count only the white keys from middle C to the octave C. You'll find eight tones which comprise a diatonic scale. "Ahah!", you might say. "I've heard the dulcimer is just like the white keys of a piano". Well, yes—but no, also.

A diatonic scale is comprised of whole steps and half steps. On the piano keyboard, C to D is a whole step because you skip the black note in between. Using the keyboard diagram on the previous page, count the whole steps and half steps between middle C and the C above (white keys only). You'll find the five whole steps and two half steps in the following pattern:

whole step, whole step, half step, whole step,
whole step, whole step, half step.

This pattern creates a major or Ionian scale. "Ionian" is an old word for the scale we call "major" today.

Look at D just above middle C on the keyboard. Move to the D above using the whole step, whole step, etc., pattern. This time you will touch two black keys—F♯ and C♯. Look at your dulcimer fretboard beginning at the 3rd fret. Disregarding the 6½ fret should you have one, move your finger along to the 10th fret, noting the small and large fret spaces. When you go through a large space, you're moving a whole step; through a small space, you're moving a half step. See the pattern emerging:

whole step, whole step, half step, whole step,
whole step, whole step, half step.

There are other scales—some in more common use than others.

Playing only the melody string, start at the 1st fret and move to the 8th fret. You have played a pure minor or Aeolian scale. Beginning once more at the 1st fret, slide along to the 8th fret noticing the pattern of whole steps and half steps. You'll again find five whole steps and two half steps, but the pattern this time is:

Aeolian	whole step, half step,
or pure	whole step, whole step
minor:	half step, whole step
	whole step

Following is a chart showing the whole steps and half steps for scales beginning at each fret (except 6½, of course) on your dulcimer.

ws = Whole Step
hs = Half Step

Scale	*Pattern*						
Aeolian (PureMinor) Frets 1 - 8	ws	hs	ws	ws	hs	ws	ws
Locrian Frets 2 - 9	hs	ws	ws	hs	ws	ws	ws
Ionian (Major) Frets 3 - 10	ws	ws	hs	ws	ws	ws	hs
Dorian Frets 4 - 11	ws	hs	ws	ws	ws	hs	ws
Phrygian Frets 5 - 12	hs	ws	ws	ws	hs	ws	ws
Lydian Frets 6 - 13	ws	ws	ws	hs	ws	ws	hs
Mixolydian Frets 7 - 14	ws	ws	hs	ws	ws	hs	ws

The scales begin again with Aeolian at the 8th fret and continue until you run out of frets! Knowing that, does it make sense that the Mixolydian Scale also begins on the open string of your dulcimer? Check out the scale pattern.

Before we continue, I'd like to tell you something interesting about the Locrian Scale. You'll sometimes read that the Locrian Scale is never used in folk music. Much of the reasoning lies in the pattern for the first five tones of the scale. Adding the half steps found in the first five tones of the scale (half step, whole step, whole step, half step), you'll find six. Try adding the half steps in the first five tones of the rest of the scales and you'll find seven. This might not seem significant, but it is. The Locrian Scale has an *imperfect* fifth interval which has been called the Devil's Interval. The other scales have *perfect* fifth intervals. Centuries ago the church had vast influence on the music of the times. Naturally, melodies smacking of the Devil were greatly frowned upon and simply weren't written. You will, however, find tunes using the other scales with major and minor being the most common.

Now we'll answer the question of *why* dulcimer players retune. Strumming *all* of the strings on your dulcimer, play from the 3rd to the 10th fret on the melody string, tuned as we have been since the beginning of the book. The drones are harmonious with the melody and tunes using that tonality (centering around the dulcimer's 3rd fret) would sound just fine. Now play a minor scale on the melody string—1st to the 8th frets—strumming all strings. This time discord is evident and something must be done. You can in many instances use chords and individual melody notes to sweeten such a tune rather than retune the instrument. But, retuning isn't too difficult and we've now reached the point of working in another tonality.

You have only one string—the melody string—to retune. We are currently tuned D A A. The A on the melody string will be raised in pitch to C.

Tune from   D A A to   D A C

Caution: be sure your melody string will reach the higher pitch. Tune slowly, testing the string to see if it is too tight. You may have to lower your bass and middle strings to accommodate the higher pitched melody string. The bass string fretted at the 6th fret will produce the pitch you need on the open melody string.

Play the minor scale on the melody string from the 1st to the 8th fret strumming all strings. Now the minor scale sounds harmonious with the drone string. But—if you now play the major scale from the 3rd to the 10th fret, we're unharmonious again. This brings up an interesting and sometimes frustrating point.

You'll see dulcimer *tunings* referred to as Ionian, Mixolydian, etc. Most often the tunes to be played do not use the scales mentioned as tunings even though one would assume they would. A prime example is the versatile D A D tuning usually called Mixolydian. Most of the melodies played in D A D are simply Major or Ionian tunes—especially if the dulcimer has the 6½ fret. Compare the patterns for Mixolydian and Major Scales. They are similar except for the last two steps. If your dulcimer has a 6½ fret, try the following: beginning on the open melody string, play (just the melody string) to the 7th fret *skipping* the 6th fret and using the 6½ instead. You've just played a major scale. 6½ frets are added to some dulcimers to lend them more versatility. Should you want one, talk with an instrument repair person. So, if you're tuned D A D you could easily play Mixolydian tunes, major tunes and, with some chords, minor tunes.

I prefer to call tunings by the notes—D A A, for example. Please be aware that you'll often hear terms such as Mixolydian tuning. I hope you'll understand what's really happening.

There are many dulcimer tunings compatible with scales beginning all over the instrument. Feel free to devise your own tunings should you wish to experiment. Now that you're tuned D A C, a lovely tuning for minor melodies, here are some examples.

Shady Grove

Needed playing style: Light and dancing.   Strong rhythm.   Notice the tuning.

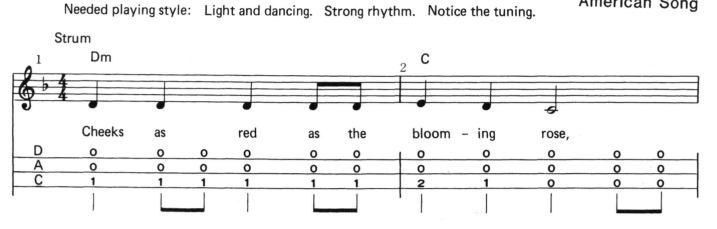

Cheeks   as   red   as   the   bloom – ing   rose,

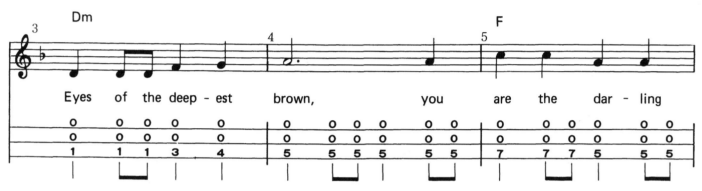

Eyes   of   the deep - est   brown,   you   are   the   dar – ling

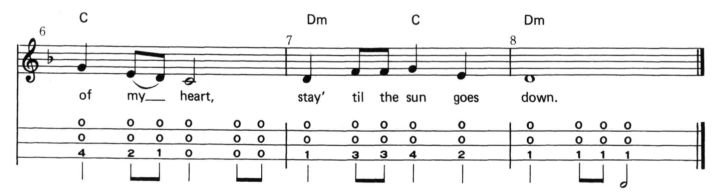

of   my___ heart,   stay' til the sun   goes   down.

Keys of F and Dm share the same key signature.
Shady Grove is in Dm.

Suggested Accompaniment Chords

O	3	6
O	4	O
1	O	3
Dm	C	F

Shady Grove, my little love,
Shady Grove, my dear,
Shady Grove, my little love,
I'm goin' to leave you here.

Shady Grove, my little love,
Standin' in the door,
Shoes and stockings in her hand
And her bare feet on the floor.

Wish I had a big fine horse,
Corn to feed him on,
Feed him when I stay at home,
Ride him when I'm gone.

Shady Grove, my little love,
Shady Grove, I say,
Shady Grove, my little love,
Don't wait 'til Judgement Day.

Greensleeves

Playing Hint: $\frac{6}{8}$ time isn't too difficult if you count out the rhythm before you begin to play.
Remember, a dotted quarter note ♩. is worth 3 beats in $\frac{6}{8}$ time.

Old English Melody

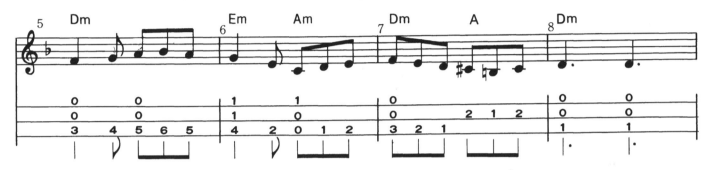

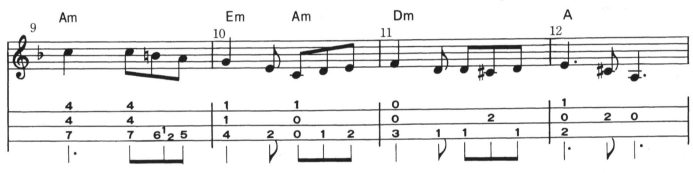

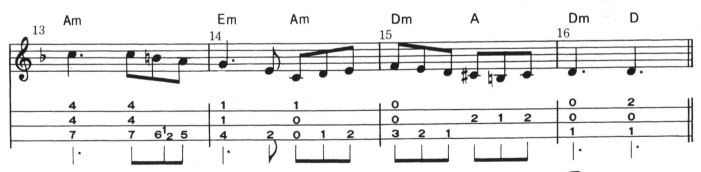

No 6 1/2 fret? play measures 9 and 13

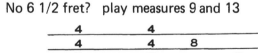

Suggested Accompaniment Chords

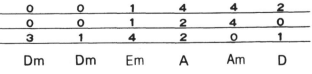

The Willow Song

Playing Hints: You may encounter problems with the rhythm, particularly the dotted quarter notes followed by eighth notes, because the keeping of the rhythm must be in your head. Perhaps you can alleviate most of the problems by carefully counting out the rhythm before you begin to play.

This version of "The Willow Song" ("O Willow, Willow") was used by William Shakespeare as Desdemona's song in OTHELLO.   Another version, with a man as the central character, is found in a manuscript in the British Museum.   The song was parodied in PLAYFORD'S PLEASANT MUSICAL COMPANION (1686) as "A poor soul sat sighing by a gingerbread stall".   The willow, by the way, is often symbolic of unhappy love.

Tune: D A C

Fingerpicked

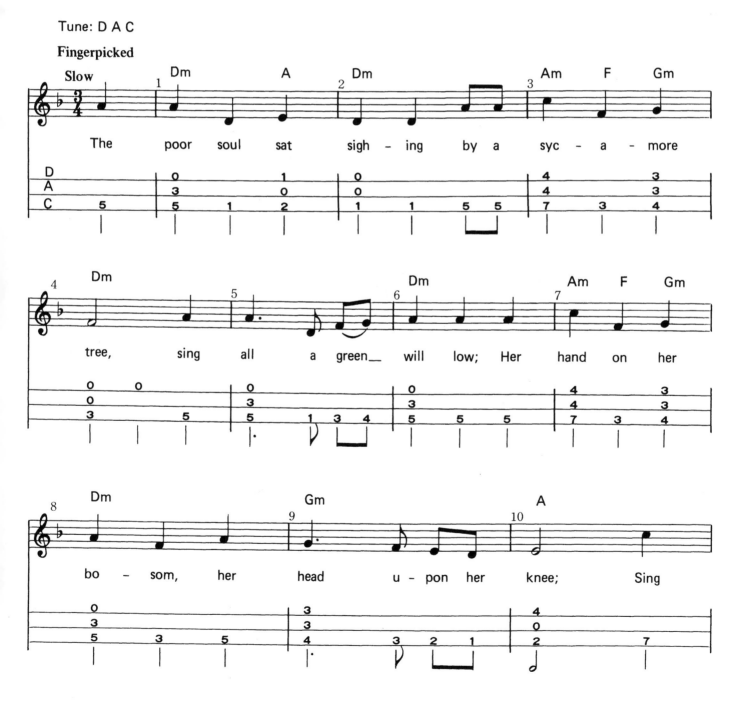

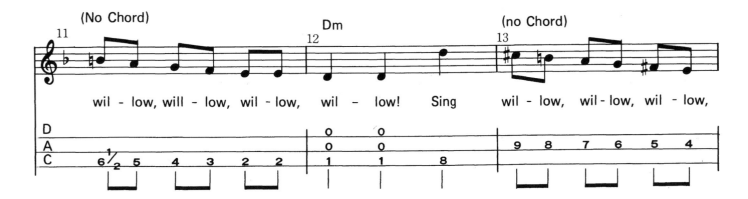

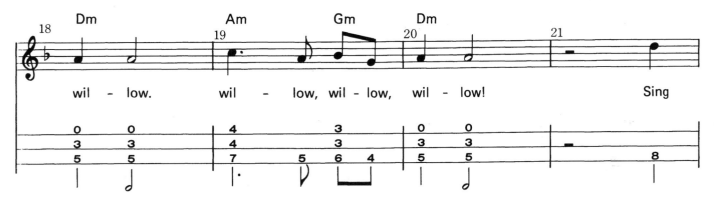

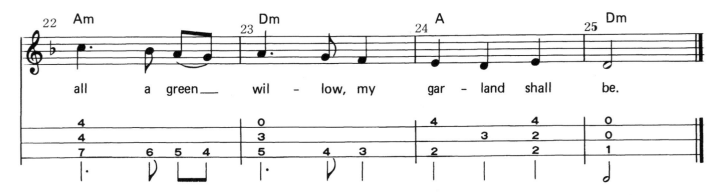

If you don't have a 6 1/2 fret:
measure 11

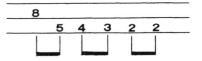

Suggested Accompaniment Chords

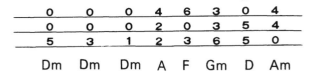

Lesson 7 D A D Tuning

Tune to D A D   —

Refer to the 7th fret on the bass string for help in tuning the melody string.

It's sometimes said that D A D is THE dulcimer tuning.   But, a tuning is a tuning is a tuning.
Later you will find yourself playing in 2 or 3 tunings which seem to fit your style. One tuning is only
better than another if it helps you achieve the sound you want.   The D A D tuning is excellent for
highly melodic playing since you have two octaves of notes in the first seven frets of the instrument.
If you're playing fast fiddle tunes fingerstyle, using more than one string, D A D tuning is almost
essential.   However, I love D A A tuning for heavily chordal playing.   Again, the choice is yours.
Just don't fall to peer pressure.

If you play in D A D a lot you should get a 6 1/2 fret if you don't already have one.   Otherwise
the necessary upper C♯ can be found on the middle string at the 9th fret.

D E F♯ G A B C♯ D

D Scale in D A D Tuning.

| | | | | | | or | | | | | | | 9 | |
| 0 | 1 | 2 | 3 | 4 | 5 | 6½ | 7 | 0 | 1 | 2 | 3 | 4 | 5 | 7 |

Before beginning any new tunes, I suggest you return to "John Brown's Dream".   It will now
sound very nice played on the melody string as well as the bass string.

Goin' To Boston

IMPORTANT STRUMMING HINTS: Because of the fast tempo of this song combined with the $\frac{2}{4}$ time signature, the strumming directions to which you're accustomed should be changed. Practice the following strumming directions.

Goin' to Boston (Continued)

This tune is true Mixolydian. It is in D (we refer to it as D Mixolydian), but the 7th tone of the scale (the C) is consistently natural, not sharped. To keep from writing each C♮, the key signature reflects this. We're brushing with another interesting music theory situation, and, because of our immediate subject in this book, I must refer you to a music theory book for more information. You can also reread the section on TUNING, RETUNING, AND WHY.

In writing down this tune, I chose a strumming style I happened to use that moment! Please memorize the melody and use your own strumming inclinations. This tune needs to be lively and danceable, since it's a play party song.

I've marked the A and B parts since I've heard this tune played A B, A A B, and A A B B. It's your decision. For a nice variation, play the tune on the bass string.

Saddle up, girls, and let's go with 'em (3 times)
Earlye in the morning.

Out of the way, you'll get run over (3 times)
Earlye in the morning.

Rights and lefts will make it better, etc.

Swing your partner all the way to Boston, etc.

Johnny, Johnny, gonna tell your Pappy, etc.

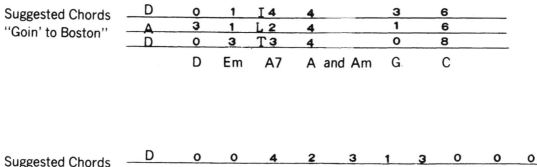

72

Bonnie Tyneside

Scottish Waltz
arr. Seth Austen

Tune: D A D

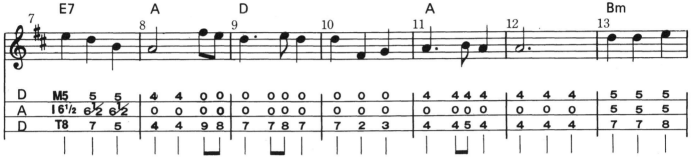

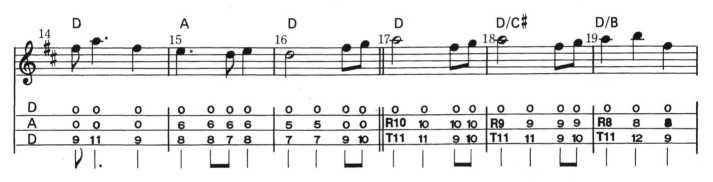

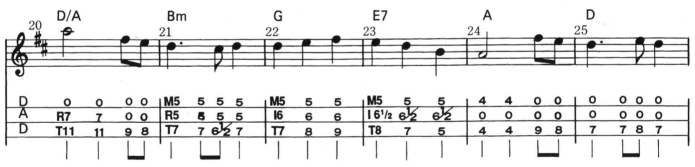

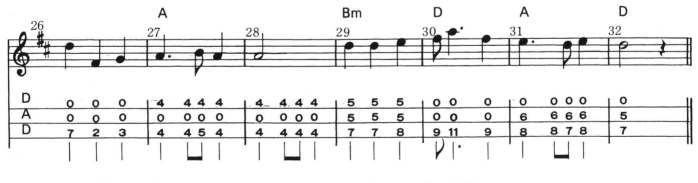

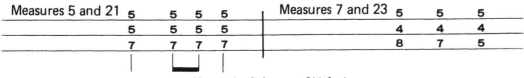

If you don't have a 6½ fret.

73

Lesson 8

Using a Capo

Forget what you know about guitar capos. Guitars have a chromatic fretboard while the dulcimer has a diatonic fretboard. Therefore, when you put a capo on a dulcimer you throw off the pattern. But first you might like to know what a capo is. It's a device which creates a nut at perhaps the 1st or 3rd or 4th or whatever fret of your choosing, thereby shortening the vibrating string length and raising the pitch of the open string. A hand-crafted capo will probably cost you about $7.00.

Chances are you won't find one in your local music store. Your best bet is to contact a company specializing in dulcimers or acoustic musical instruments. If you have any problems, contact me at DULCIMER PLAYERS NEWS and I will help you. You can fashion your own capo from a chopstick attached to the dulcimer with a large, heavy rubber band.

Let's examine what happens when you place the capo at the 1st fret in a D-A-d tuning. Strumming the open strings produces the notes E-B-e, and the tonality centers around these notes. However, if you place the capo at the 3rd fret, the open strings produce G-D-g and the tonality settles there. Capoed at the 1st fret in the D-A-d tuning, you can easily play in the key of E minor; capoed at the 3rd fret in D-A-d, you can easily play in the key of G major. When you capo at the 4th fret, you can play in the key of A minor by using the 6th fret and A major by using the 6½ fret.

Things change a little when you capo using the D-A-A tuning. Capoed at the 1st fret, you can easily play in E Dorian. Dorian and Aeolian (the pure minor scale) are very similar. The pattern for Aeolian is whole step, half step, whole step, whole step, half step, whole step, whole step. The pattern for Dorian is whole step, half step, whole step, whole step, whole step, half step, whole step. The E minor (Aeolian) scale has the following notes: E, F♯, G, A, B, C, D, E; the E Dorian scale has E, F♯, G, A, B, C♯, D, E. In comparing the E minor and E Dorian scales, you'll notice that the differing note is C. In the minor scale, the C is natural; in the Dorian scale the C is sharped. If you look at the capoed arrangement of "When Johnny Comes Marching Home," you'll notice that this tune has no C in it. Thus, we can use the capo at the 1st fret in either the D-A-d or D-A-A tuning and play the tune. I used the D-A-A tuning since all of "When Johnny Comes Marching Home" can then be played on the melody string. You can use the capo at the 1st fret in D-A-d tuning if you'd like to work the tune out by ear. The melody begins on the open melody string and you will need to use the middle string for some of the tune.

Capoed at the 3rd fret in the D-A-A tuning, you can play in the key of G major, but your scale runs as follows:

```
  0  4  5  6
              0  4  5  6
 _____
  G  A  B  C  D  E  F#  G
```

You can begin the G scale on the melody string at the 6th fret, but at the 9th fret you'll find a C♯ instead of the C♮ you need for the scale. This works fine with the capoed arrangement of "She'll Be Coming 'Round the Mountain" because no C—natural or otherwise—is used in the melody of the tune.

If you decide to use the capo extensively in your playing, I suggest you tune your open strings to D-A-d.

Experiment with a capo some, especially when you feel comfortable with other tunings. You might find a unique sound!

Let's try a capoed tune in D A A. Please remember that fret numbers remain the same. If you're capoed at the 1st fret, fret number 2 is still called 2 even though it's now the first fret after the capo. But the open strings are

       0   1

designated 0 rather than 1 . I hope I didn't lose you there!

       0   1

She'll Be Coming 'Round The Mountain

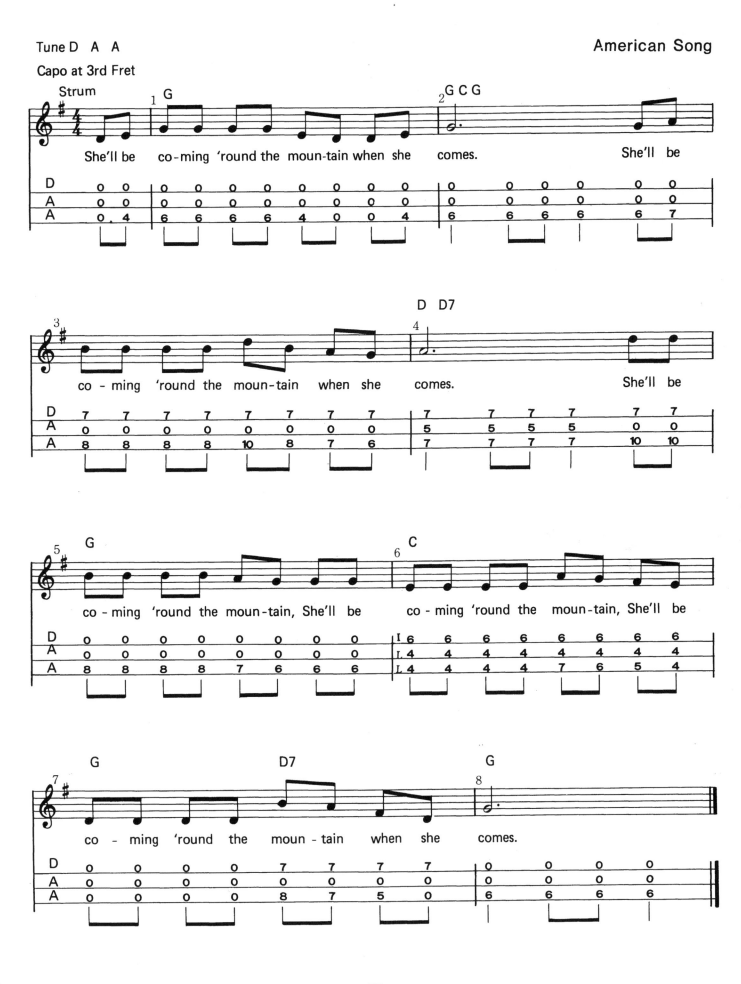

Home on the Range

Tune D A D
Capo at 3rd Fret
Fingerpicked

When Johnny Comes Marching Home

The strum is critical to the total sound here. The pick continually goes as follows: ↑↓↑.↓↑↓

out, in, out - in, out, in. The first two measures have arrows drawn in.

Lesson 9

Playing While Others Play

There is a tradition to keep when playing fiddle tunes and other instrumentals. I suggest you don't confuse—or perhaps ire—a fiddler or other musician by suggesting he or she play all tunes in your favorite key. Many of the Appalachian, Irish, British, Canadian and Scottish tunes are traditionally played in D, G, or A—and you can handle most of the necessary chords in one of two ways:

1. becoming adept at playing two or three keys in one tuning,
2. becoming adept at using a capo.

Playing More than One Key in One Tuning

The keys of D (2 #'s), G (1 #), and A (3 #'s) are closely related. Comparison:

Key of D:	I	Chord is D		Key of G:	I	Chord is G
	V	Chord is A			V	Chord is D
	V^7	Chord is A^7			V^7	Chord is D^7
	IV	Chord is G			IV	Chord is C
	VI	Chord is Bm			VI	Chord is Am
Key of A:	I	Chord is A				
	V	Chord is E				
	V^7	Chord is E^7				
	IV	Chord is D				
	VI	Chord is F#m				

See how many chords are shared by the keys? Only the position of importance is chanced. For example, a D chord is a I chord in the key of D, a V chord is the key of G and a IV chord in the key of A.

Following is a chart for a D A A tuning showing some chords in tablature for various keys.

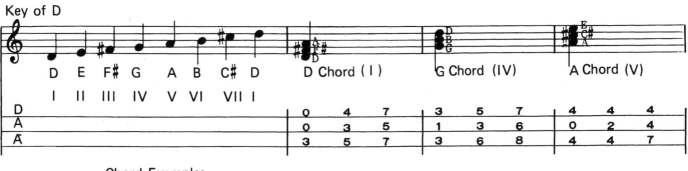

Chord Examples

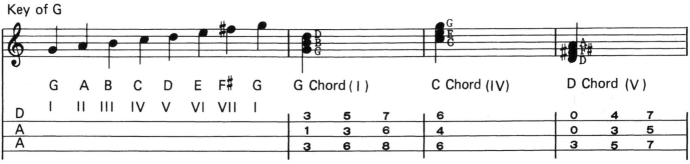

Chord Examples

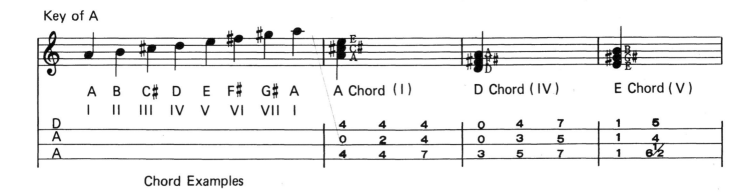

Chord Examples

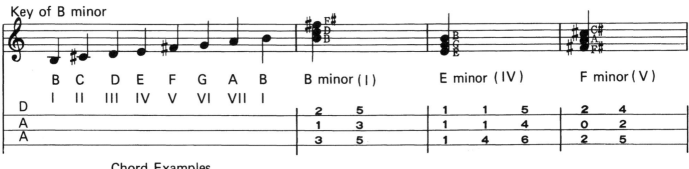

Chord Examples

The chords on the previous page were merely examples. You can find many more chords by drawing your fretboard with the notes in its current tuning. You have to know the notes that make up each chord and remember that you can change position of the notes (F# rather than D on the bass string in a D chord, for example), double notes, or leave out notes. Since we've played so much in the D-A-A tuning, try your hand at figuring out some chords in the D-A-d tuning. Below is a picture of the fretboard in that tuning. Look for D chords (D, F#, A), A chords (A, C#, E), A7 chords (A, C#, E, G), G chords (G, B, D), Bm chords (B, D, F#), and Em chords (E, G, B). They'll take you through a lot of tunes.

There's one thing to remember about the A7 chord (or any 7 chord, for that matter). Four notes make up the chord and you probably have only three strings on your dulcimer. What notes do you choose? Since the A7 is a form of an A chord, it's nice to have the A. The G is the note which makes it an A7 chord, so you should really have that note. Choose between the C# and the E as your remaining note by deciding which is easier to reach and which gives you the sound you want. It really dresses up a tune to be playing an A chord in the key of D and them moving to the A7.

Chart for D A D Tuning

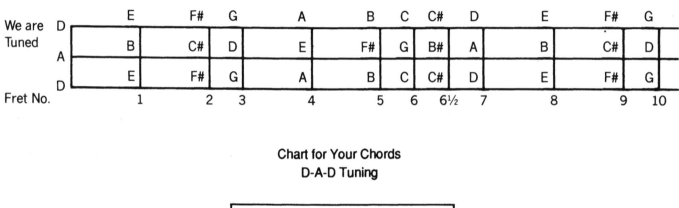

We are Tuned		E		F#	G		A		B	C	C#	D		E		F#	G
D																	
A		B		C#	D		E		F#	G	B#	A		B		C#	D
D		E		F#	G		A		B	C	C#	D		E		F#	G
Fret No.		1		2	3		4		5	6	6½	7		8		9	10

Chart for Your Chords
D-A-D Tuning

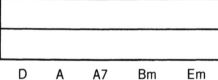

D A A7 Bm Em

Now you need some cooperative friends to play other melodic instruments. I'd suggest a fiddle, tin whistle or hammer dulcimer. Of course, be sure to invite instruments such as guitar and autoharp which often play harmony but are good on melodies. Get the other musicians to go through the chord structure of a tune with you first and then proceed to play through the tune numerous times. I will write out two D tunes so you can play melody or harmony.

Following is a tune in D. Try both the melody and the harmony. If there's no one else to play with you, tape the melody and accompany yourself.

Whiskey Before Breakfast

Fiddle Tune

Strum

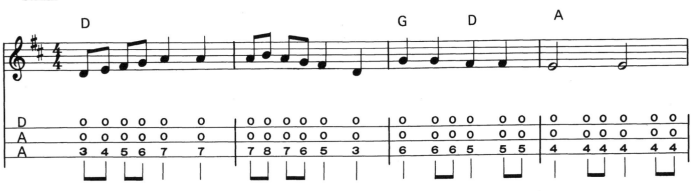

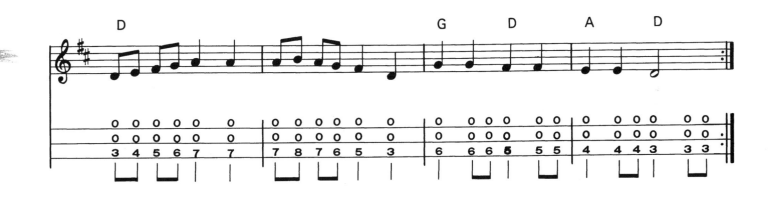

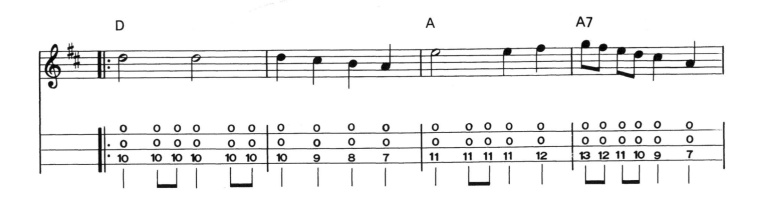

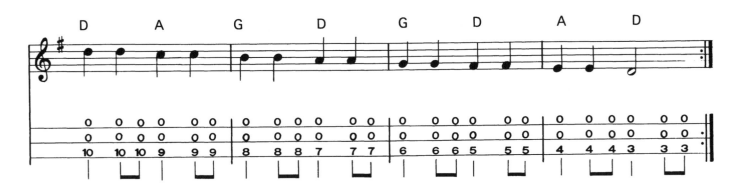

Lesson 10

Using a Noter

You might find the placement of this lesson strange. After all, isn't playing with a noter easier than doing fancy left-hand finger work? Perhaps—but good traditional noter work is spirited and wonderful. It is a technique worth exploring when you feel comfortable with your left-hand work.

You can purchase beautiful noters of exotic wood or make your own. My favorite noter is a Popsicle stick. You can play in one of two ways:

1. Thumb on top, other fingers curved by fretboard, or
2. index finger on top (little less control).

The noter glides over the melody string(s) while other strings are played open. Practice some tunes in the book such as "Soldier's Joy" and "Goin' to Boston" and enjoy the "whooshing" sound as the noter glides over the strings. I encourage you to incorporate a noter into your playing when old-time traditional tunes would be enhanced with that sound.

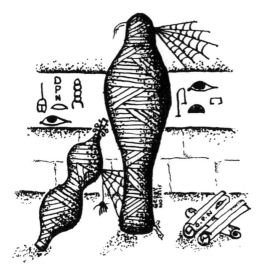

Lesson 11

Changing Strings

It's a temptation to leave strings on a dulcimer until they break. You might actually find your instrument sounds brighter and more alive if you change strings now and then. It's hard to say when now and then occur—every 6-8 weeks or so.

If you've just changed strings and you break one, just replace the broken one. However, if your strings have been on for some time, change them all. Your bright new string might otherwise get lost in the plunky sound of the old ones.

Please don't call your dulcimer strings banjo strings as is often done. Although the two instruments use similar strings, a string is just a musical string. If you put it on your dulcimer, you then have a dulcimer string. If the string goes on a banjo, *then* it's a banjo string.

Strings are purchased by size in thousandths. Before going to the music store, study the strings you have.

Some dulcimer strings have a loop which slip over little nails on the tail piece of the instrument. Other strings have ball ends. Determine the type of strings you need.

Typical dulcimer bass strings range in size from .028 to .018. (The larger the number, the larger the string.) Bass strings are usually wound (a core wire is wrapped with another wire). Run your fingernail over your bass string. If it "screeches" it's wound.

This is the time to consider your vibrating string length. If the dulcimer has a long vibrating string length (say 30″) and you select a large string (say .026), your pitch will be lower than if you have a shorter string length. Everything is relative.

Other dulcimer strings are usually not wound.

They typically range in size from .014 to .009.

The nut and bridge of your dulcimer were built to accommodate certain strings. If you purchase one appreciably larger, it may not fit in the slots cut in the nut and bridge. If you purchase one that is appreciably smaller, the string may vibrate in the slots producing a buzzing sound. If you're changing strings for the first time, you may have to experiment to find the strings which suit your dulcimer and your playing wishes.

Following is a suggestion for stringing:

Bass string: .022 wound
Middle string: .013
Melody string(s):   .012

Caution: When changing strings for the first time, be sure to study the string you remove to see how it fits on the peg.

A musical string on an instrument has a pitch that is just right for the particular vibrating string length. But this string can be pitched higher or lower by several whole tones.

As you and your instrument grow in friendship, you'll learn which strings and which pitches fit your instrument best.

Harvest Home

Irish Tune
arr. Seth Austen

Strum

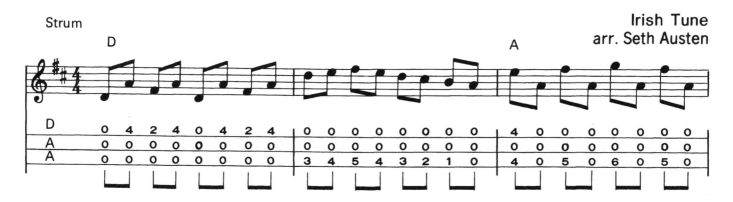

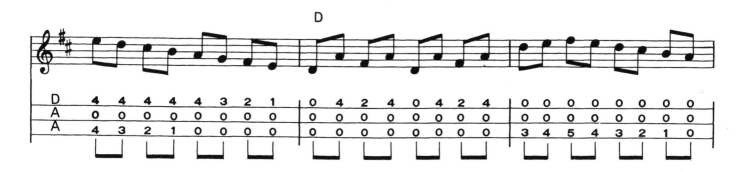

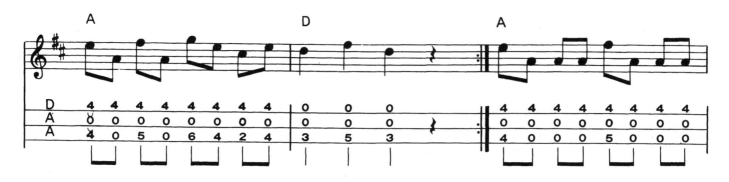

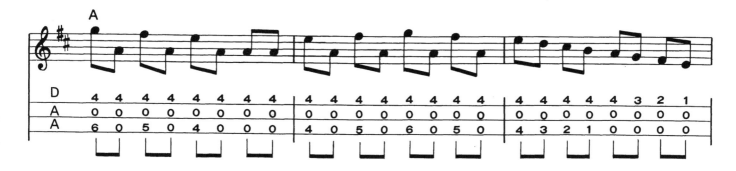

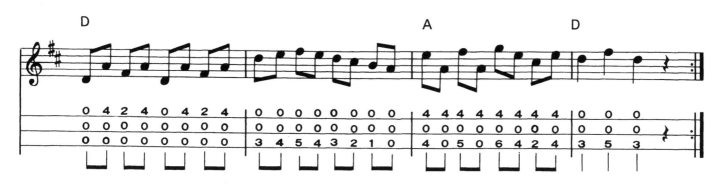

Lesson 12 Interpretation

Interpretation is difficult to talk about in concrete terms. I'll give you some suggestions and ideas, but most creativity must come from you. I've sometimes told someone how lovely a tune sounded, only to see a lowering of the head and an embarassed, "Oh, I just play at it" . Please get those thoughts out of your mind. If I really believed you just played to keep from cleaning the garage, I wouldn't have written this book. The creative urge is in all of us - it just comes out in different ways (quilting, managing budgets, teaching, drawing, etc.) as well as music. You must trust your creativity and listen to the tiny voice inside you which says a fast tune would be nice played slowly with embellishments. Still trust even when everyone else plays it differently. Try something, believe in it awhile and see what happens. Perhaps you've discovered something. Perhaps later you'll go back to playing it fast - but with a special difference since you tried something new.

Hammer - ons and pull-offs are interpretive tools. They create a different sound. First, how they're played:

1. Hammer-on - place your middle finger at the 3rd fret. Leave it there, pluck the string and then drop your index finger assertively at the 4th fret (don't pluck again) . For one pluck you get two notes.

2. Pull-off - you now have two fingers down (middle and index) at the 3rd and 4th frets. Pluck the string, then pull off the index finger (don't twang) . Notice I said pull off. Don't just lift off or you won't get much sound.

Exercise: Combining hammer-ons and pull - offs:

Fingering: Use ring, middle and index fingers, work for smoothness

H = Hammer -- On   P = Pull - off

D
A | H | H | P | P | P | | H | H | P | P | P | | | H | H | P | P | P |
A | 4 | 5 | 6 | 5 | 4 | 0 | 4 | 5 | 6 | 5 | 4 | 0 | | 4 | 5 | 6 | 5 | 4 | 0 |

| H | H | P | P | P | | 4^H | 5^H | 6^P | 5^P | 4^P | 0 | | 4^H | 5^H | 6^P | 5^P | 4^P | 0 |
| 4 | 5 | 6 | 5 | 4 | 0 | | | | | | | | | | | | |

If you're having trouble getting the feel of hammer-ons and pull-offs, try the following: using your ring, middle and index fingers, pretend you are playing hammer-ons on the soundboard of your dulcimer. Hammer enough to hear the thump of your fingers. Then curve your fingers and pull off each finger, one by one. You should hear your finger scrape against the soundboard. Try this several times before putting your fingers back on the strings.

85

Following are two tunes which example hammer-ons and pull-offs. But you've already had examples—you just didn't know it. The idea of hammer-ons and pull-offs is smoothness of playing in addition to the particular sounds they give. Basically, whenever you have ascending notes on any strings hammer-ons are options with any or all of the notes.

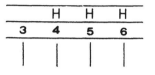

When you have descending notes on any strings pull-offs are options.

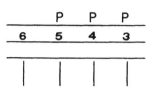

That is true whether you strum or fingerpick. When do you choose the hammer-on, pull-off options? When *you* think they enhance the music or make the notes easier to play. Practically every tune in the book has a spot or two for hammer-ons and pull-offs. Look at a few tunes you play fairly well and decide where these techniques might be useful.

I warn you that the following arrangement of "Harvest Home" is not easy, but your efforts will reward you with a fine tune. It uses hammer-ons and pull-offs on most of the notes. Use only your index, middle, and ring fingers. If you learned the earlier arrangement of "Harvest Home", compare the sounds of the two. They're both nice, just different. Two striking differences are the tunings (D A A, D A D) and the right hand style (strumming, fingerpicking).

Harvest Home

Irish Tune
arr. Seth Austen

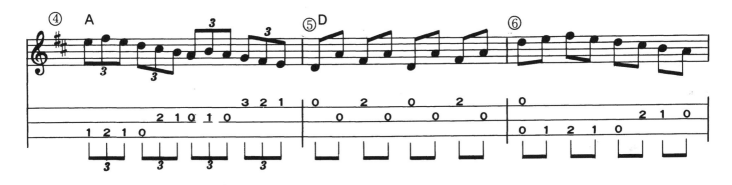

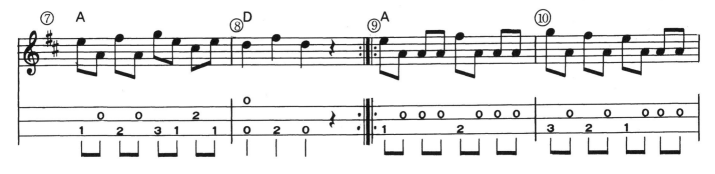

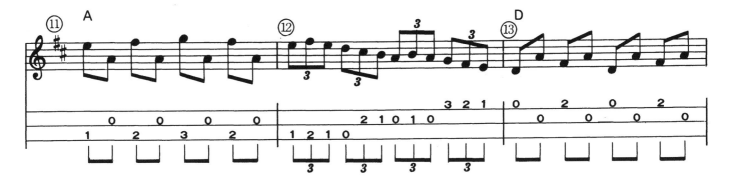

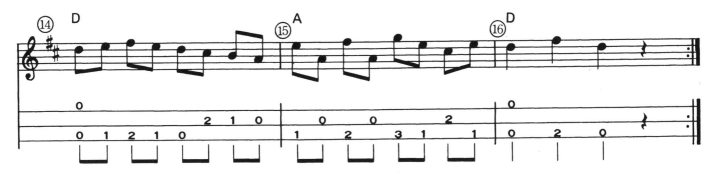

Country Gardens

"Country Gardens" also uses many hammer-ons and pull-offs.

This tune should dance.   It moves rather quickly, but not too fast.

English

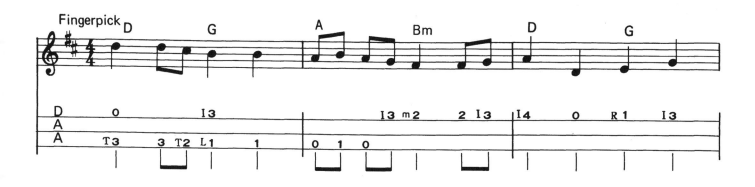

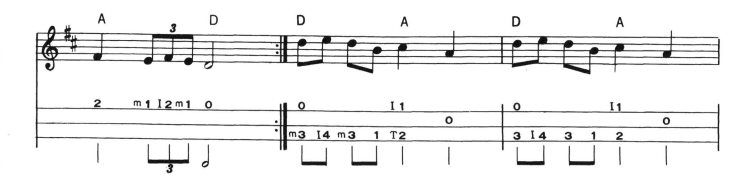

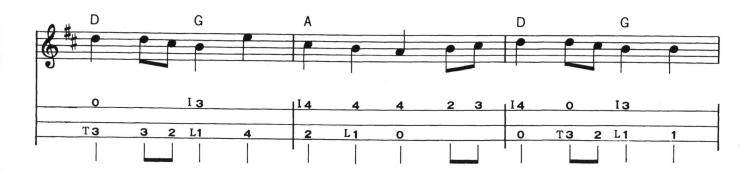

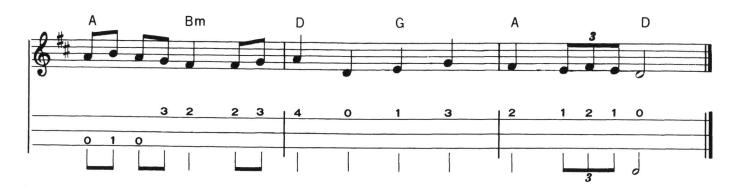

Please note: Musical notation is written one octave higher than tablature.

Interpretation usually means little things. A note left out or played differently can sparkle up a tune after it's been played several times. For example, look at measure 2 of "Flop-Eared Mule"—the first chord. Instead of strumming when your little finger is at the 1st fret, pull-off with a slight twang. Remember not to strum that chord. The difference perks up your ears. Just remember to vary what you do when tunes are repeated. Measure 16 of "Flop-Eared Mule" also has a possibility. Instead of strumming through both chords,

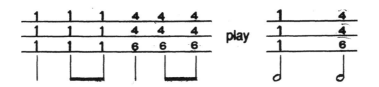

Since you've consistently strummed, this small change perks up the ears.

Remember: Interpretation doesn't only mean adding things in. Leaving things out works also. Interpretation doesn't mean having to be fancy, just creative.

Harmonics

If you've ever read directions for blowing bubble gum, the following will rival them. Bear with me.

Harmonics (sometimes called "chimes") are so lovely. Think of them as the clock chimes in "Grandfather's Clock" or as the lovely tones you couldn't decifer at the end of an occasional tune. Harmonics are overtones of the notes on the open string. To create them, you touch a string lightly (don't press down), pluck the string, and release your touch. The easiest spots to find the harmonics on the dulcimer are *on* (notice it's "on," not "by") the 7th, 4th, 3rd and 5th frets. The sound is unmistakable; so, when you have the touch just right, you'll know. Practice putting some 7th-fret harmonics at the end of some of the tunes and songs in this book.

The following two arrangements work with interpretation by layering (duets with dulcimers in different tunings), volume changes, and suggested right-hand variations.

Ah Poor Bird, Hey Ho, Rose Red

Playing instructions: By this time you'll probably think these rounds are simple to play . . . no chords, no fancy rhythms . . . . You're correct in ways, but we're going to make this round practically *sing* itself. The best approach is by singing the rounds one at a time until everyone feels comfortable with them. Want to try singing them as rounds? They're beautiful.

Have you ever considered the similarities between singing and playing? If you play as if you're singing (observing "breathing" spots, volume, etc.), you should feel as if you can hardly resist opening your mouth and bursting into song. I'll act as choral director in the following observations:

Ah, Poor Bird

Volume: Crescendo (gradually get louder) through the word "sorrows" and then decrescendo (gradually get softer).

Breathing: Do <u>not</u> breathe (keep the strumming going) throughout the line, "Ah, poor bird take thy flight" and again through "far above the sorrows of this sad night".

Hey, Ho, Nobody Home

Move your strumming arm to the right toward the bridge for a crisp sound.   Fairly loud volume throughout.   No "breath" during "meat nor drink nor money have I none".

Rose Red

Strum over strum hollow area.   Imitate a string bass here by making sure the bass string is included in your strum. No "breath" during "I will never see thee wed".   Move closer to the bridge for "I will marry at my will sir, at my will".   This shouldn't be as loud as "Hey, Ho, Nobody Home".

Finally, to make this truly sing, move when you play.   Let feelings come through your hands. The rounds work as individual tunes or as a unit by playing through all three songs before beginning again with "Ah, Poor Bird".   When one voice begins the 3rd measure, the next voice enters.

Interpretation: Lo, How a Rose E'er Blooming

If you have longish fingernails on your right hand, you can achieve two sounds; a rather crisp, nail-produced sound and a softer flesh-of-the-finger sound. "Lo, How A Rose E'er Blooming" is a good place to try this skill.

This beautiful Christmas song should have an ethereal flowing sound. Picture a choir singing it, with lots of "oh" and "oo" sounds in the beginning.

Also, we encounter rests (built in pauses in the music) that should be observed.

To stop the sound for the rest, decisively drop a couple of right-hand fingers on the string or strings. Notice the time signature. This one isn't common—the half note getting one beat—but after a little counting, you should be fine. Play using a plucked style on the three note chords—that is, pull up on all three strings at the same time (no twangs, please. Think lute!).

This arrangement has a harmony part. If you're observant as you should be, you'll notice that the melody part uses a D A A tuning while the harmony part uses D A D. Did you think that couldn't be done? The layering effect is very nice.

Lo, How a Rose E'er Blooming

Fingerpicked

Kölner Gesangbuch 1599

Moderately Slow

If you don't have a 6 1/2 fret,

play measures 2 and 11:

Isaiah 'twas foretold it,
The Rose I have in mind,
With Mary we behold it,
The Virgin Mother kind.
To show God's love aright,
She bore to men a Savior
When half-spent was the night.

Lo, How a Rose E'er Blooming - Harmony

Harmony arr. by Seth Austen

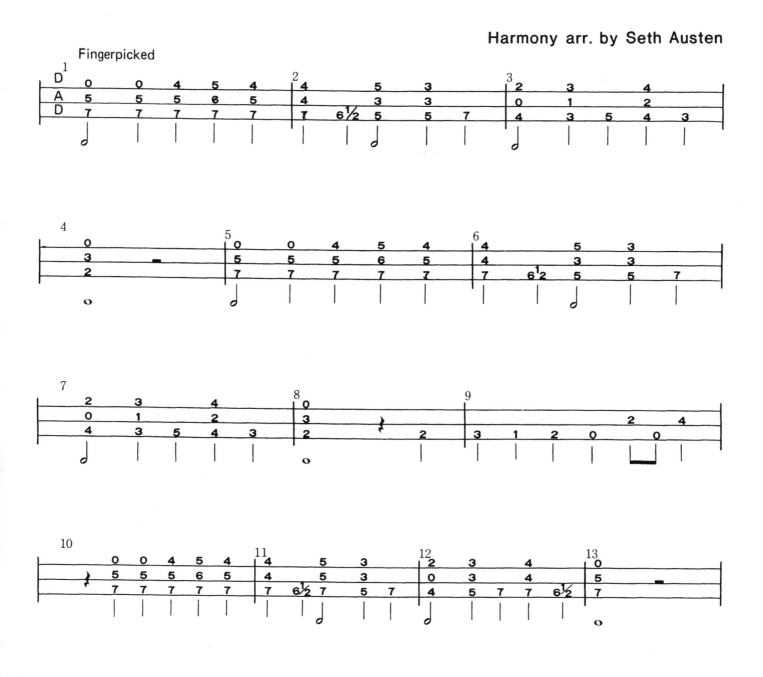

If you don't have 6 ½ fret:

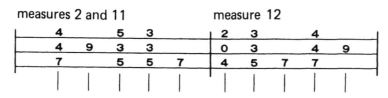

measures 2 and 11   measure 12

Where to Go from Here

1. Subscribe to DULCIMER PLAYERS NEWS. I'd be remiss if I didn't mention the magazine I publish. It will keep you in touch with people, events, and what's new. Our address is P.O. Box 2164, Winchester, VA 22601.
2. Try to attend at least one dulcimer festival. The spring issue of DULCIMER PLAYERS NEWS runs a list of more festivals than you'd imagine there would be, all over the United States. You'll find new friends, good times, and reinforcement for your music.
3. Enroll in a music class. If you'd like to know more about music in general, most colleges offer music theory and history for the layman. It's interesting how study of one kind of music enlightens you to another kind.
4. Join a folk music organization. They keep the traditions alive and can be found all over the country.
5. Listen to traditional music programs on public radio. While you're at it, become a member of your local NPR station. Your support is necessary and always welcome.
6. Attend concerts. The newsletters of the folk organizations are your best source for concert information. Hearing others play can inspire your own playing.
7. If you continue to play, consider performing for nursing homes, schools, and hospitals in your area. You will be so appreciated that any jitters you feel will quickly fade.

In closing, I'd like to tell you how this book was created. I took hundreds of thoughts, picking and choosing the ones to be incorporated within these pages. Had I written all my thoughts, the book would have rivaled Webster's unabridged dictionary in size. There's more to be said about note playing and singing and even about changing strings. But each author must be reasonable in material covered. I encourage you to sample other books—some in methods and others in specific areas such as Irish music and Renaissance melodies—for a well-rounded dulcimer education.

I'm glad I was able to share your first dulcimer moments with you. Perhaps I'll have the opportunity to hear you play some day.

Other Mel Bay Dulcimer Solo Books

20 Irish Tunes and Songs for Mountain Dulcimer in DAD Tuning (MacNeil)

A Dulcimer Christmas (Ford)

American Fiddle Tunes for Mountain Dulcimer (Hornbostel)

Anthology for the Fretted Dulcimer (Hornbostel)

Basic Dulcimer Solos (Wasburn)

Blues & Ragtime for Fretted Dulcimer (Baker)

Cajun Favorites for Mountain Dulcimer (Hornbostel)

The Celtic Collection (L. Jones)

Celtic Songs & Slow Airs for Mountain Dulcimer (Hellman)

Complete Book of Celtic Music for Appalachian Dulcimer (Nelson)

Dulcimer Duets, Rounds and Ensembles (Hornbostel)

Dulcimer Fiddle Tunes (Hornbostel)

The Dulcimer Hymn Book (Ford)

Dulcimer Jam (Carol)

Dulcimer Songbook (Ford)

Favorite Old-Time American Songs for Dulcimer (Nelson)

Folk Songs of Old Kentucky (R. L. Smith/MacNeil)

Greenwich Village: The Happy Folk Singing Days 1950's and 1960's (R. L. Smith/MacNeil)

The Irish Dulcimer (Hornbostel)

La Musica: Latin American Music Arranged for Hammered and Fretted Dulcimer (Carol)

Lullabies and Other Lilting Melodies for Dulcimer (L. Jones)

Melodies and More for Mountain Dulcimer (Einan)

Mountain Dulcimer (Biggs)

Music of the Shakers for Mountain Dulcimer (Hellman)

O'Carolan Harp Tunes for Mountain Dulcimer (Stevens)

Old-Time Hymns & Gospel Favorites for Mountain Dulcimer (Lough)

Psalms, Hymns and Spiritual Songs for Voice and Dulcimer (Irvine/Benkert)

Songs and Tunes of the Wilderness Road (R. L. Smith/MacNeil)

Southern Mountain Dulcimer (Erbsen)

Stephen Foster for Mountain Dulcimer (Stevens)

The Wonderful World of DAA (MacNeil)

WWW.MELBAY.COM